Flamingos and Sea Turtles Adult Coloring Book

This Coloring book belongs to:

_____

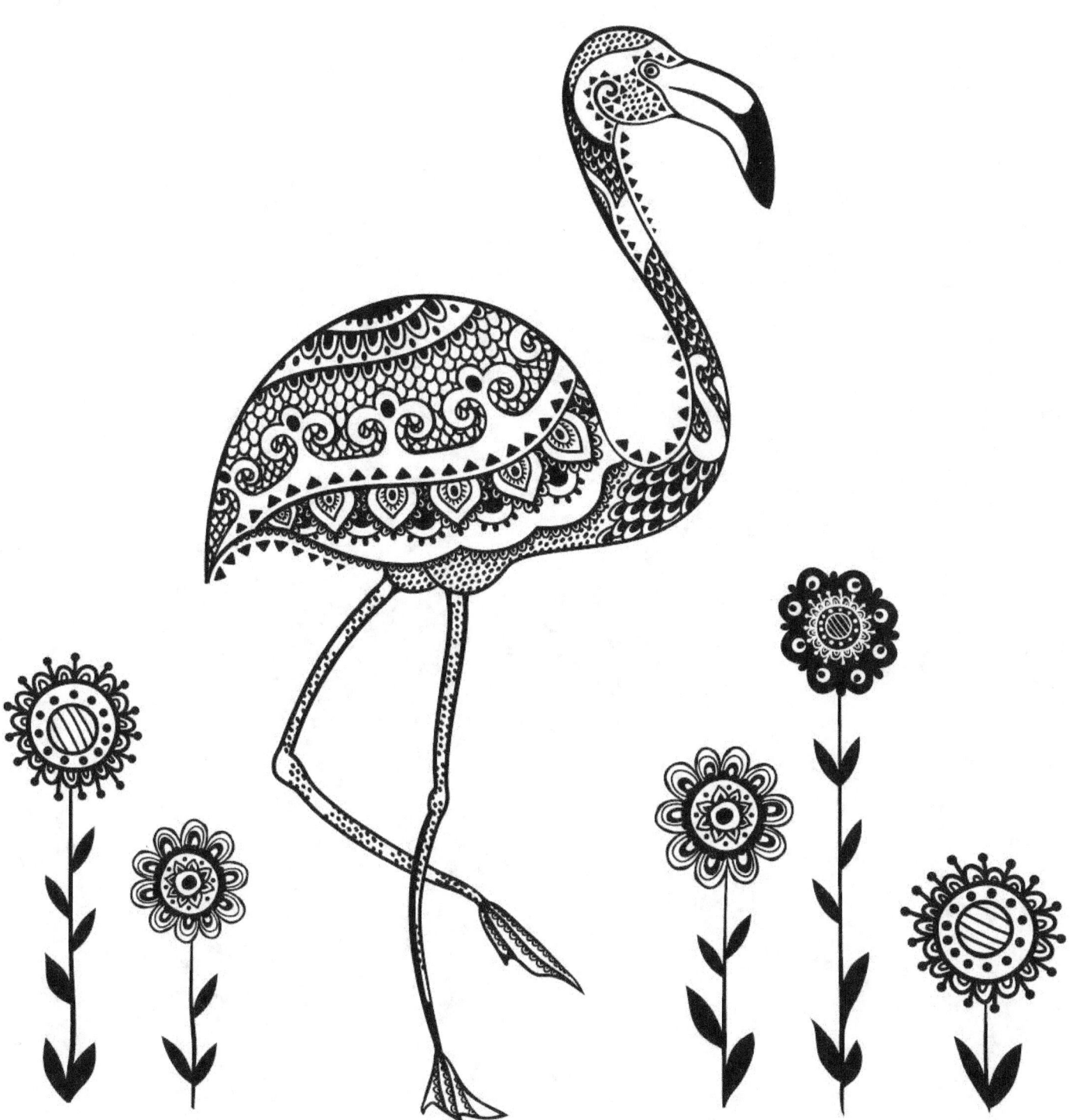

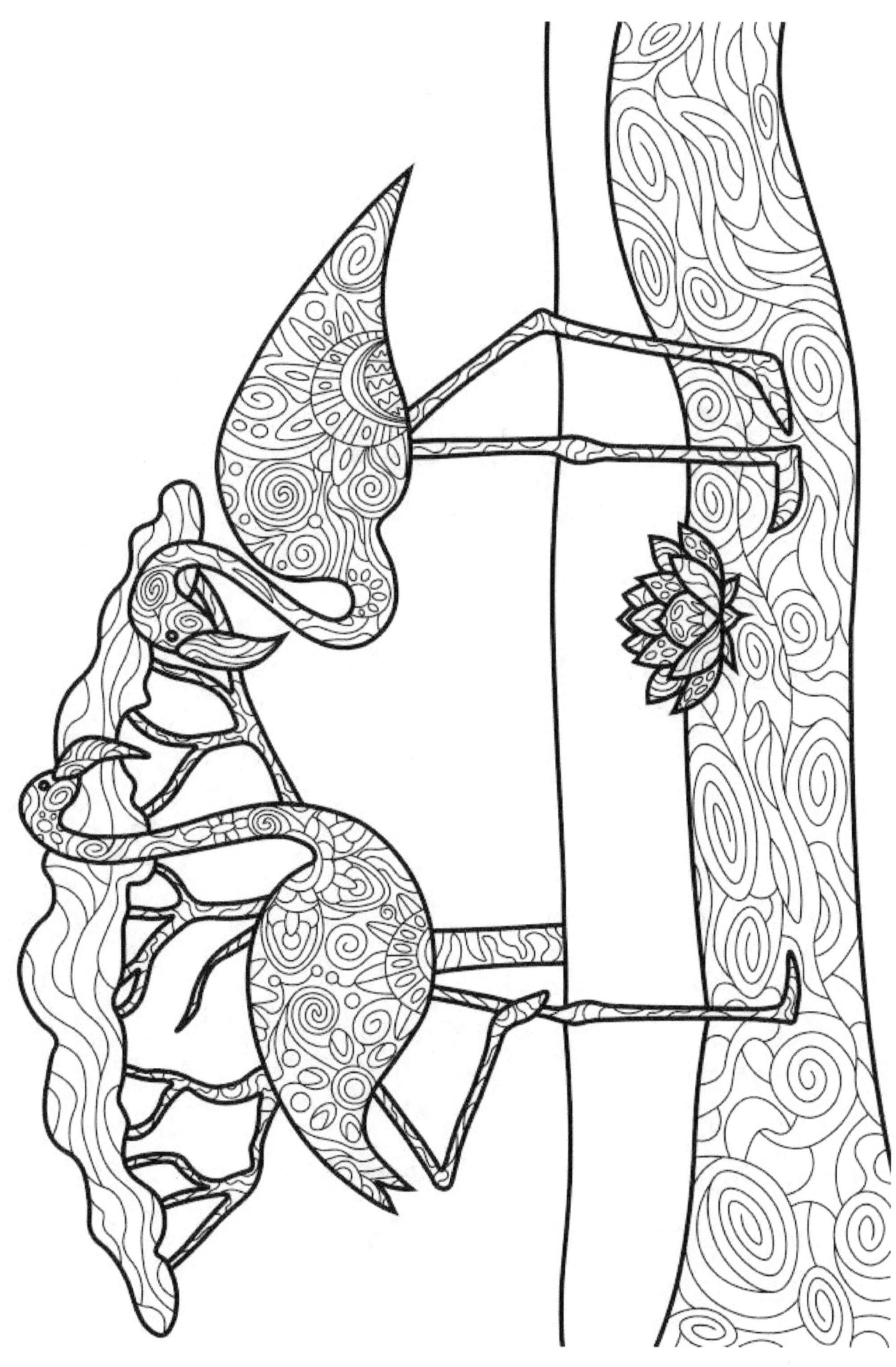

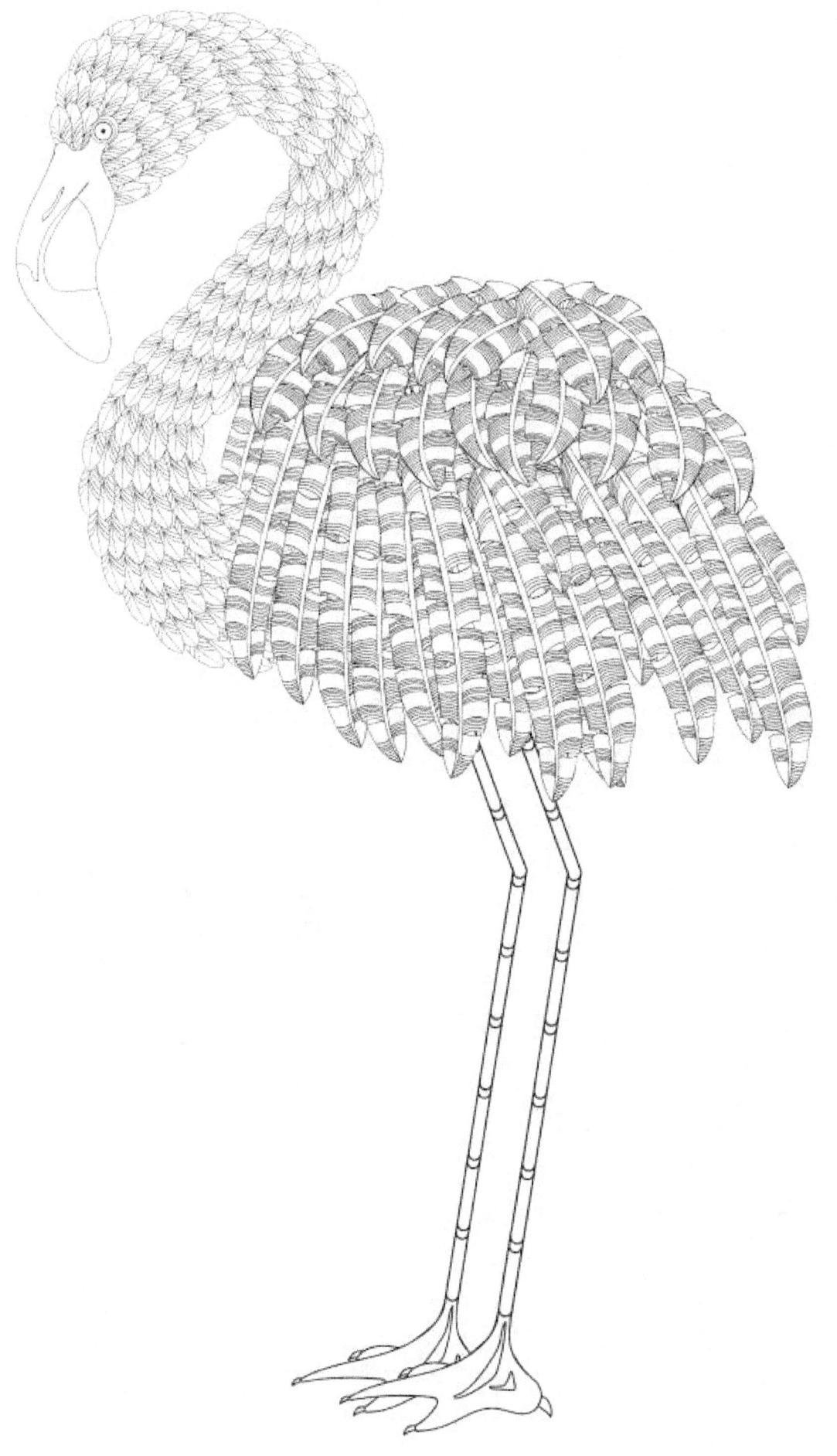

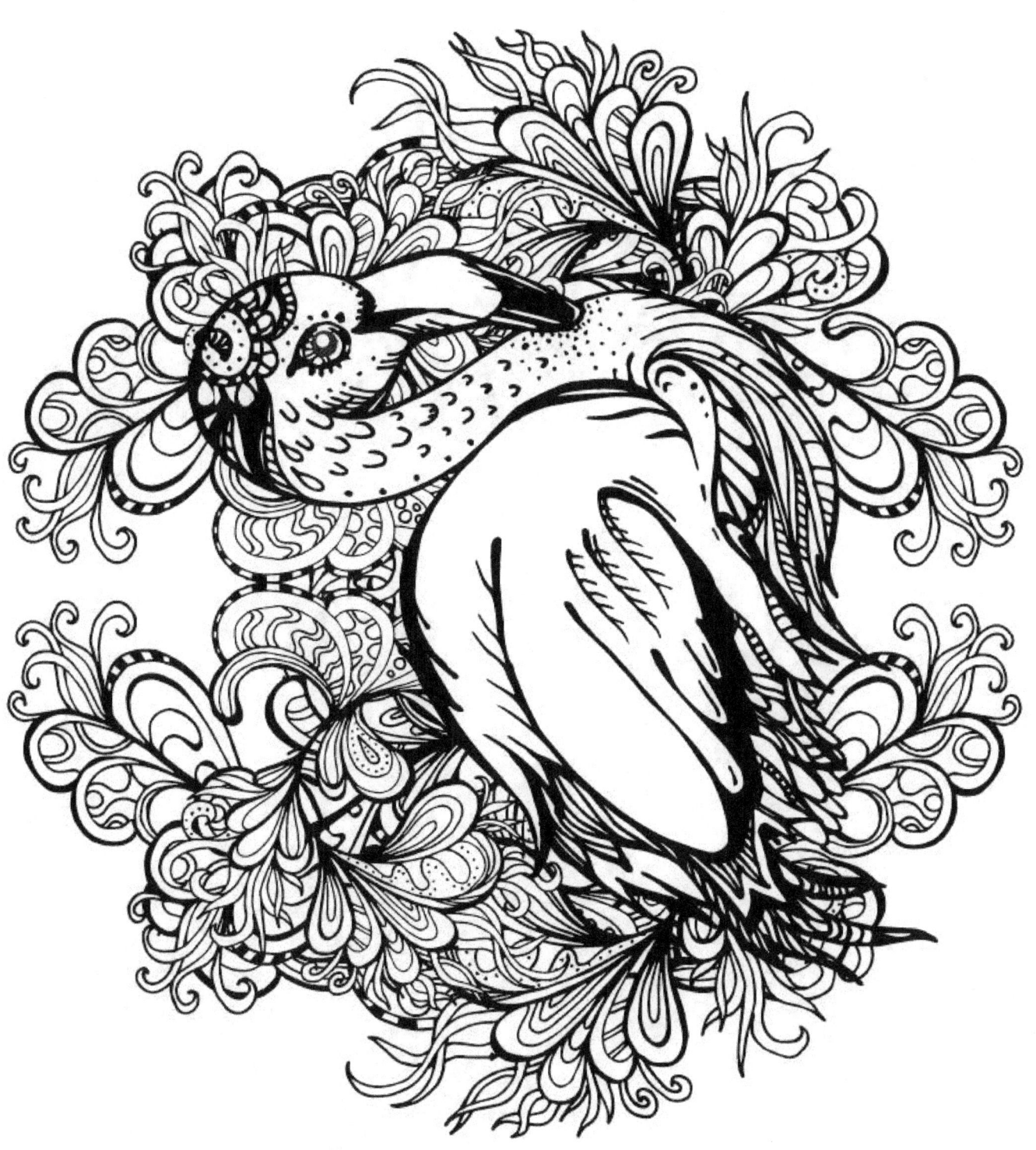

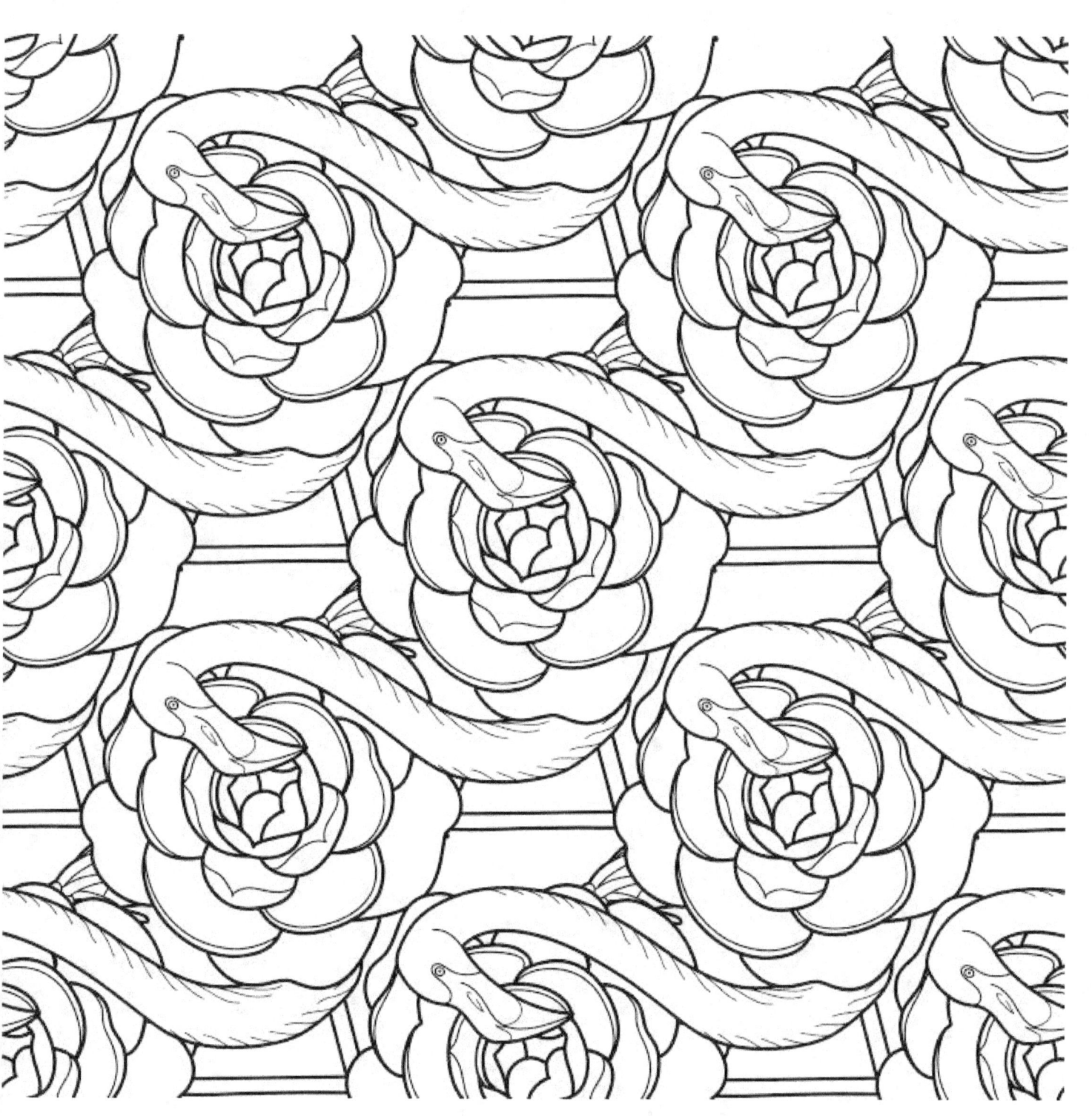

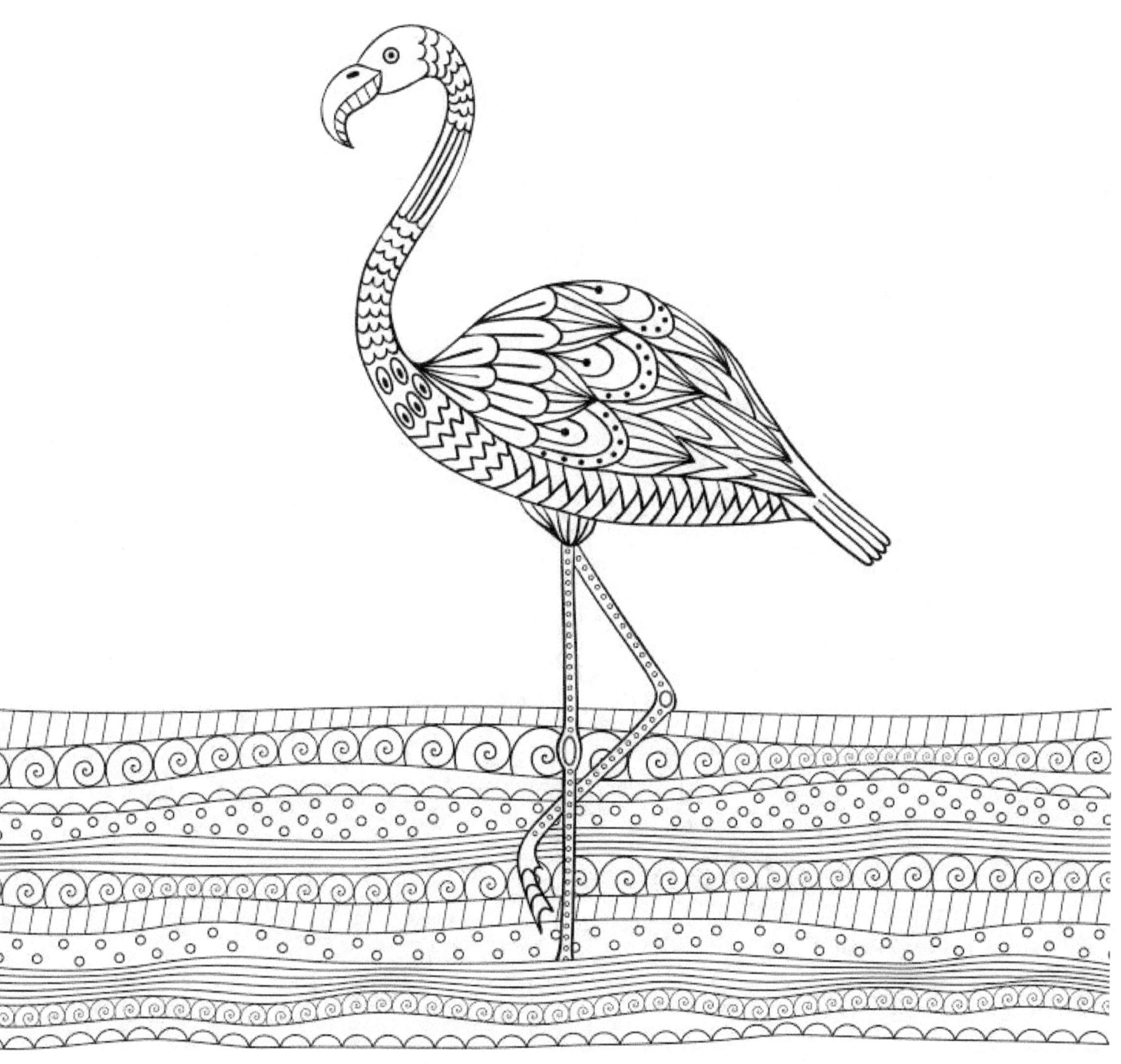

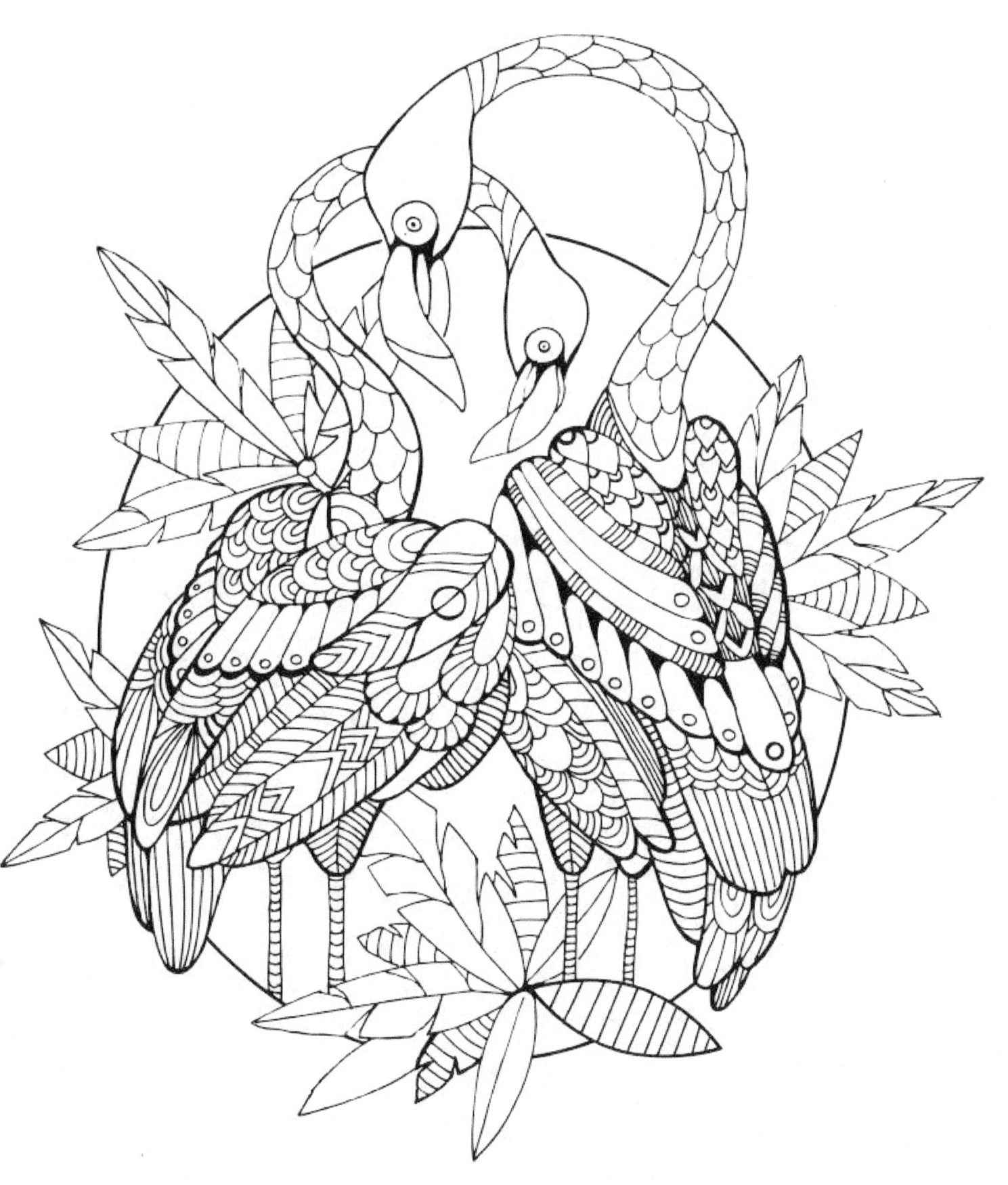

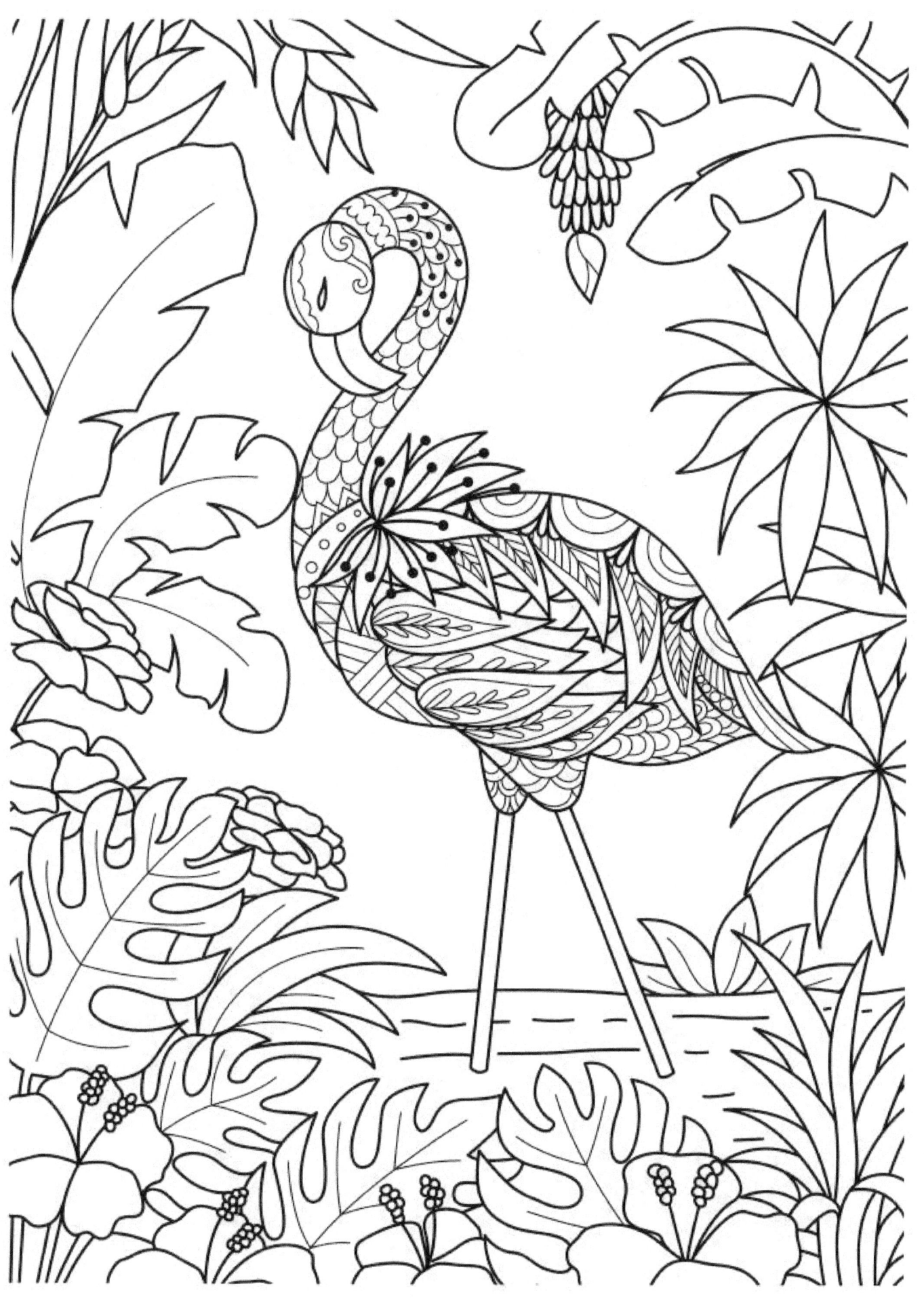

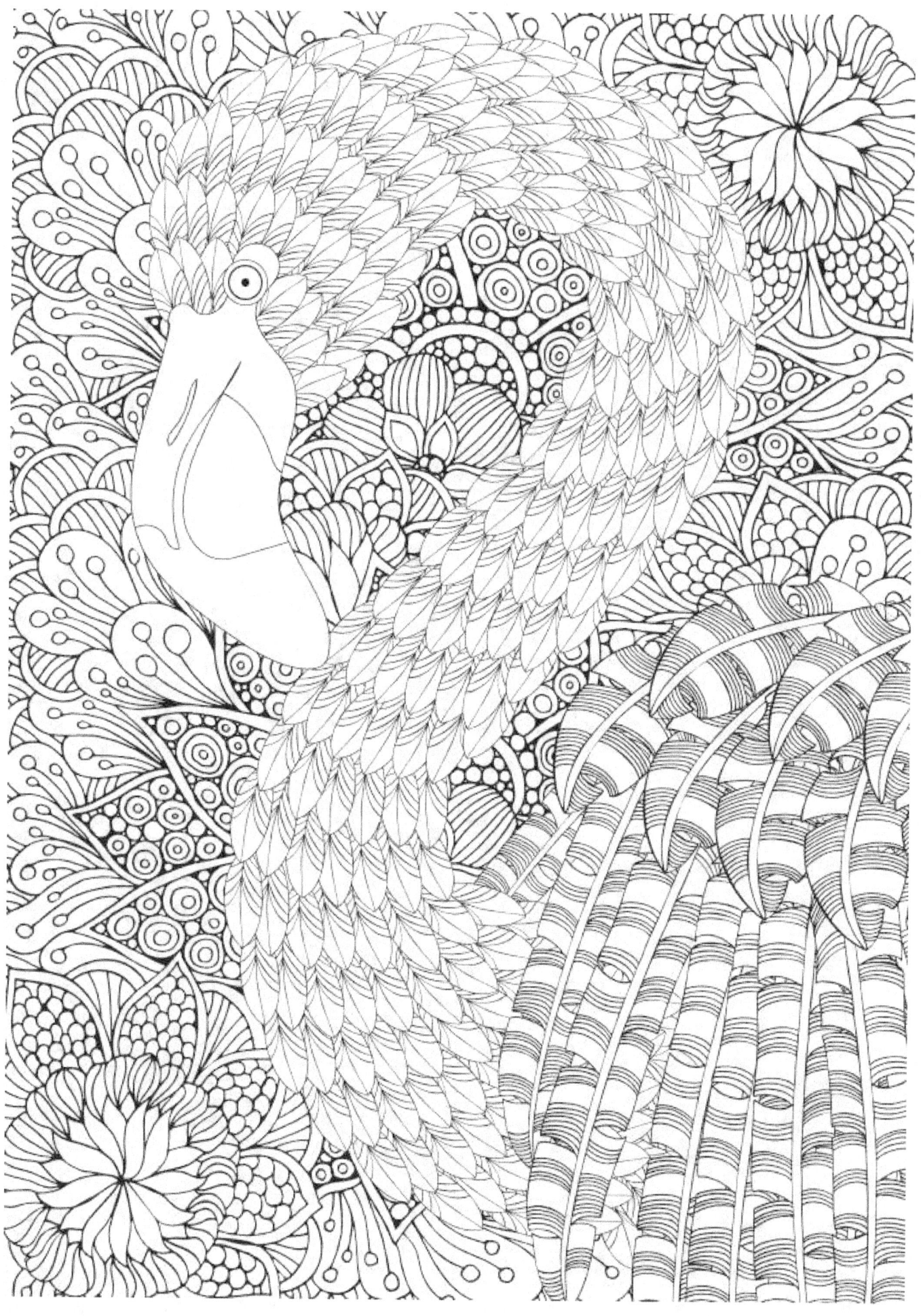

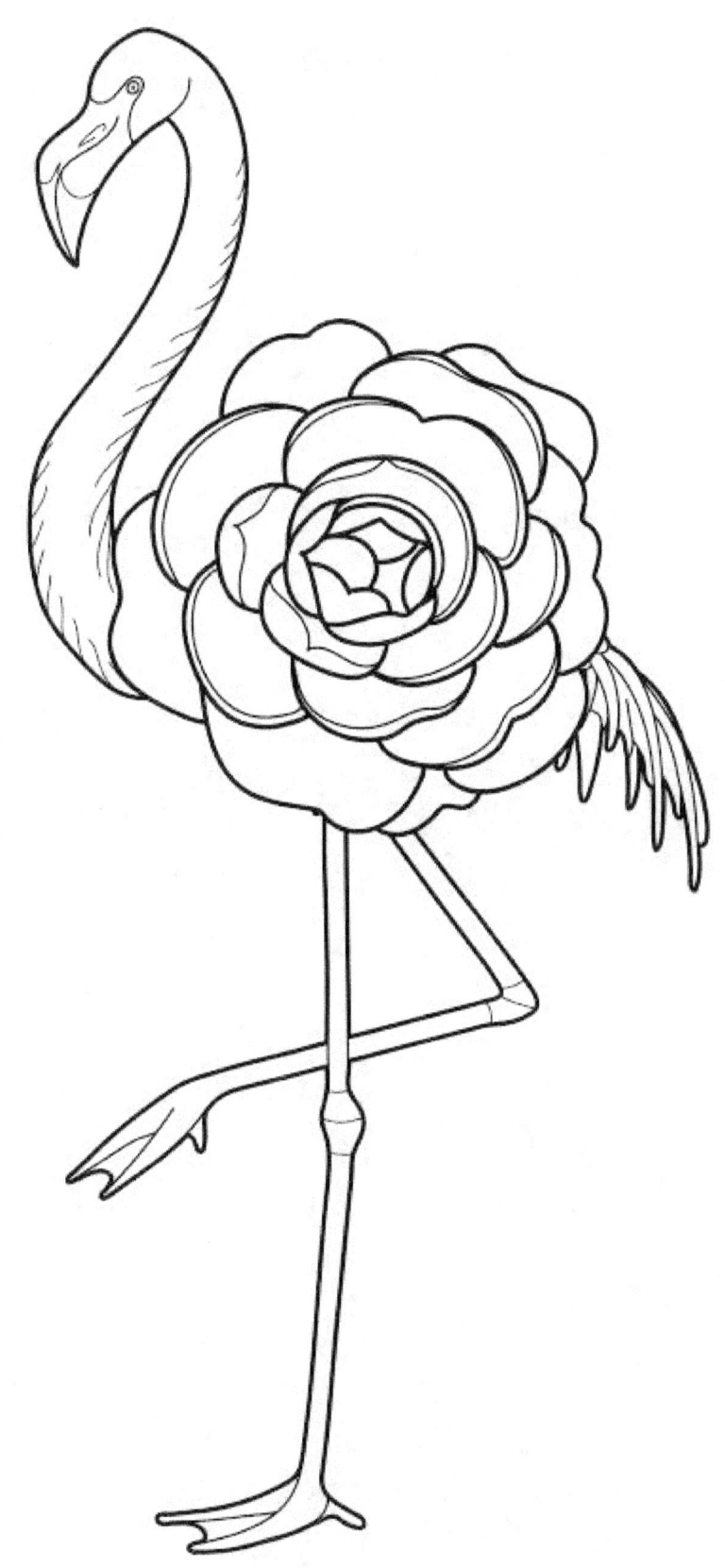

Example of different color shades to use for your flamingo coloring pages.

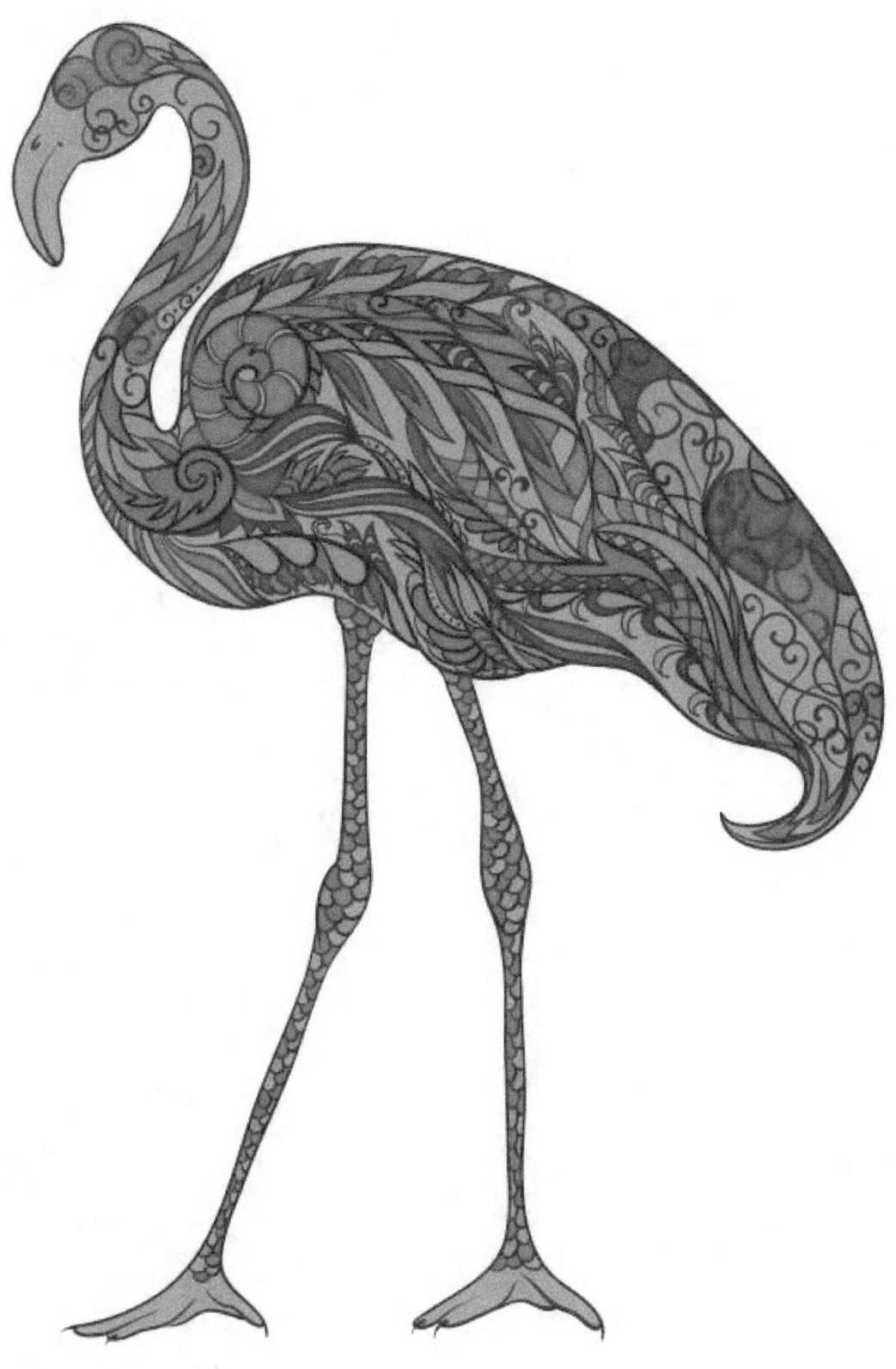

SURPRISE MIDDLE PAGES BONUS! FROGS COLOR PAGES.

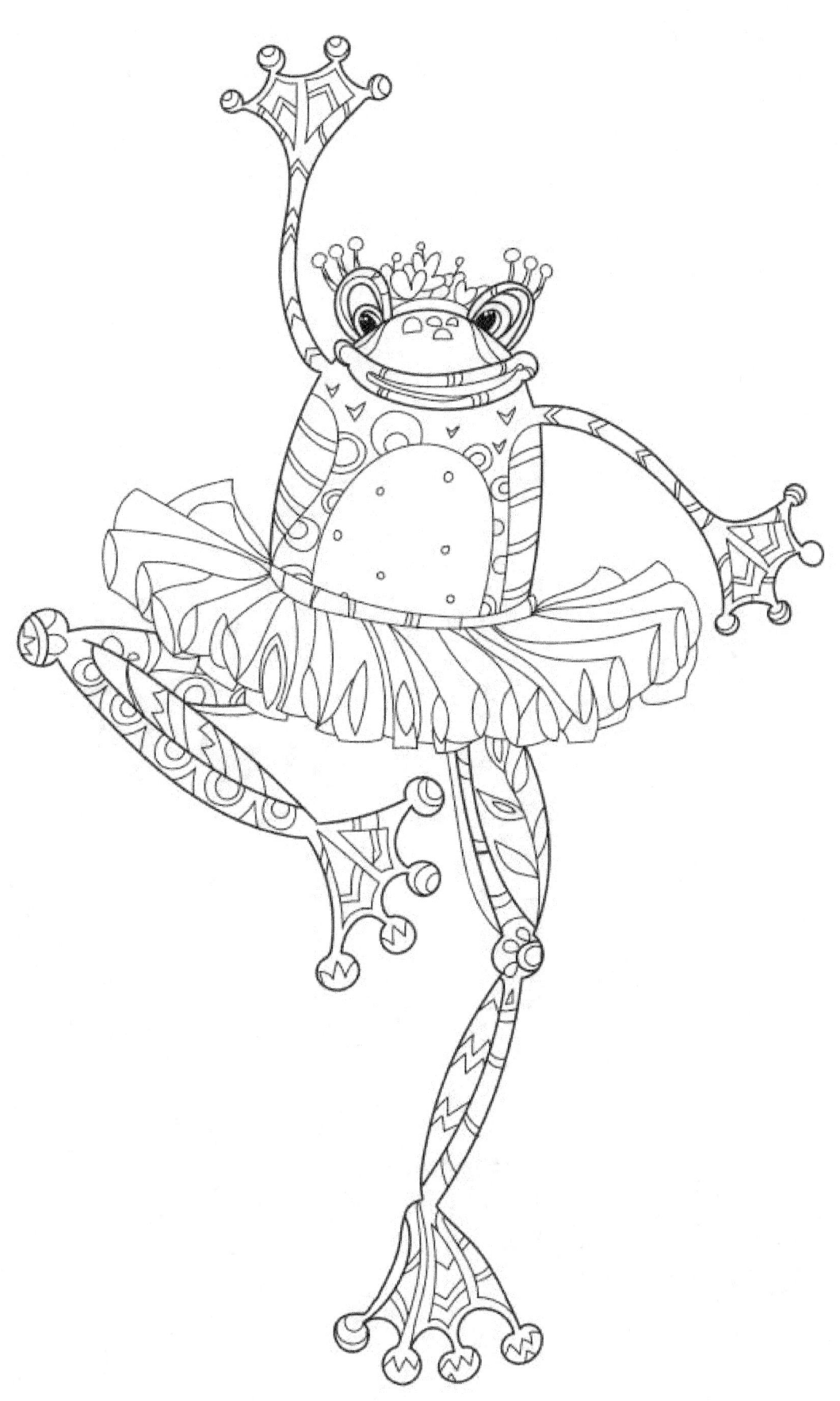

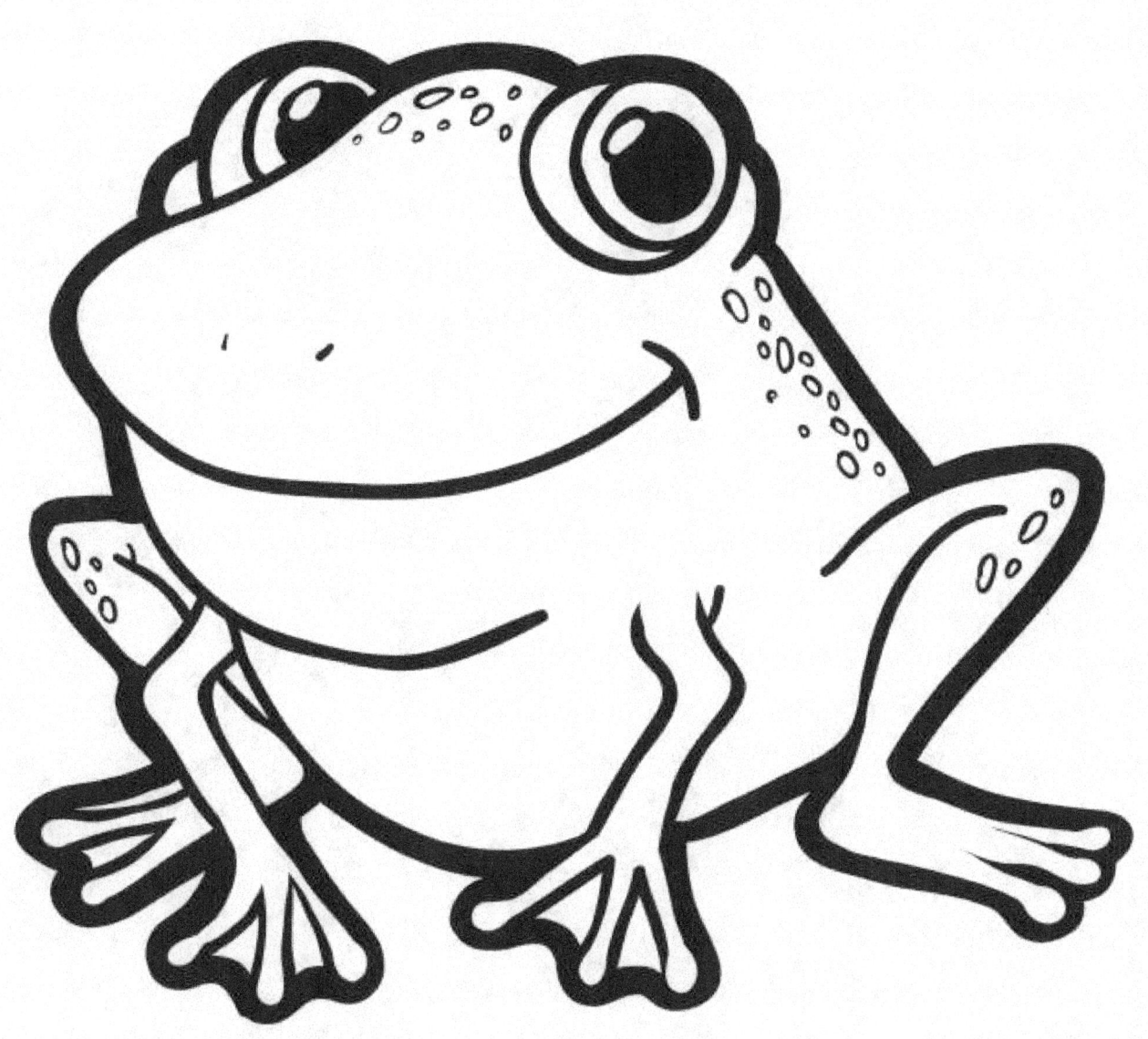

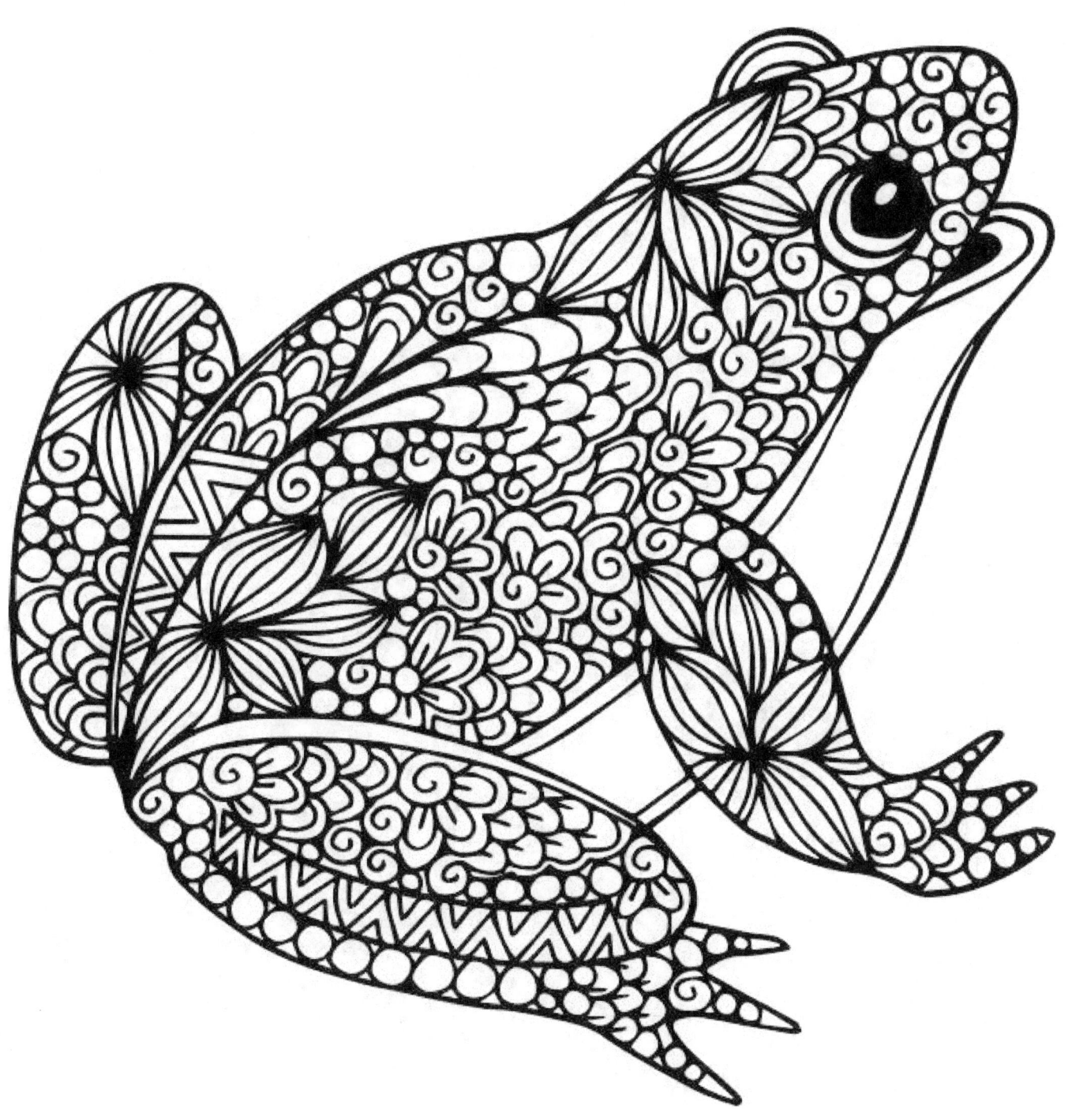

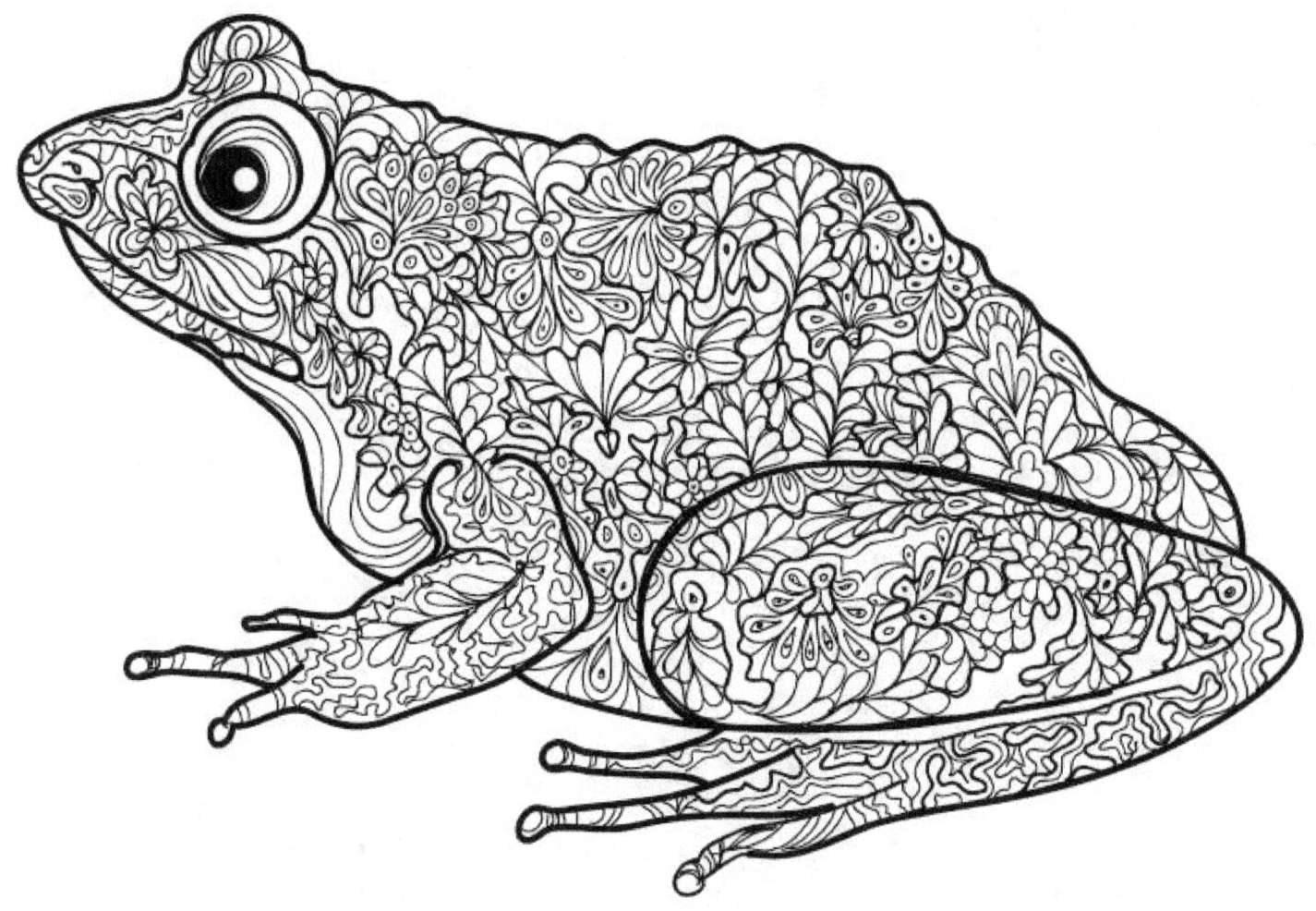

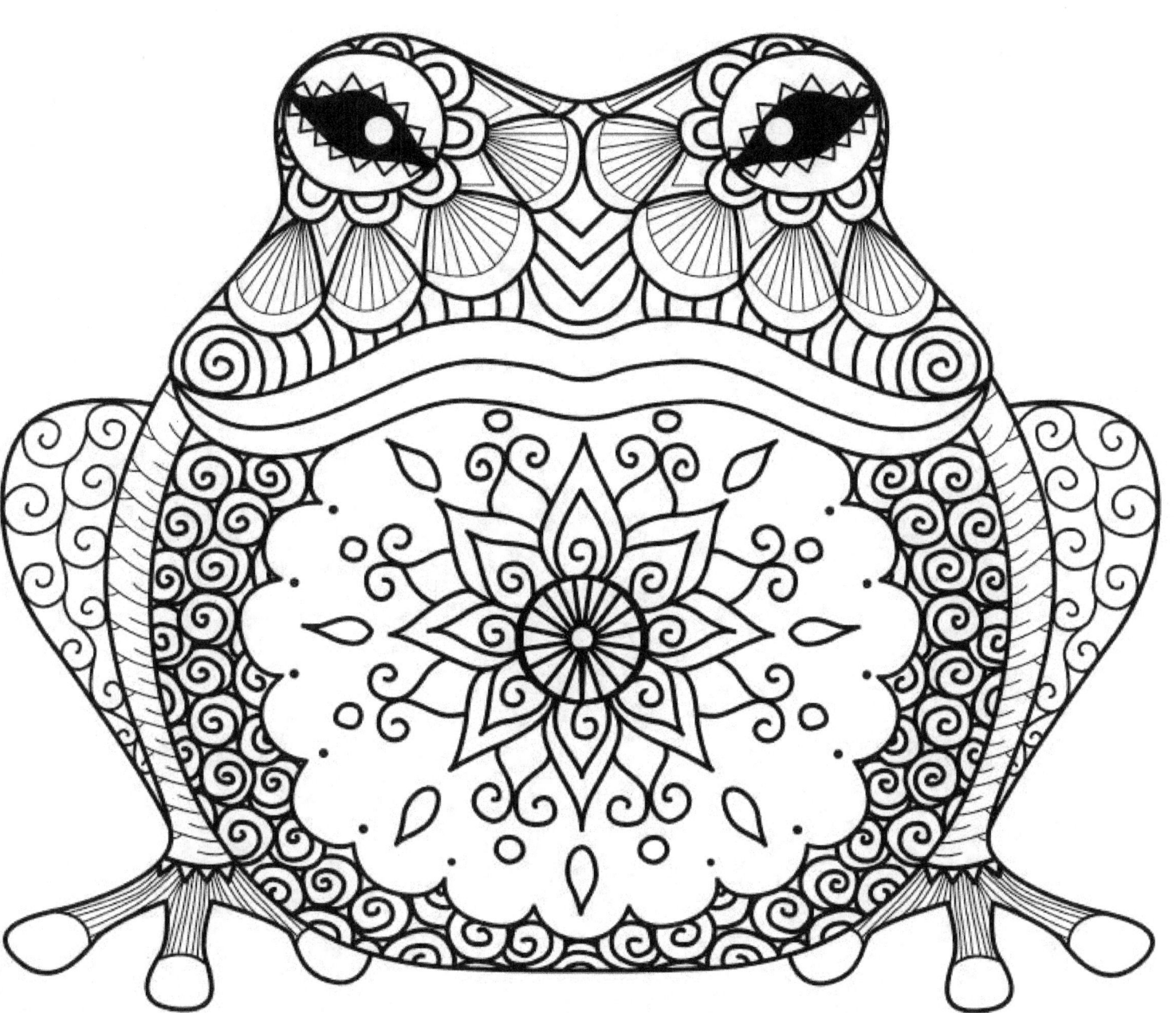

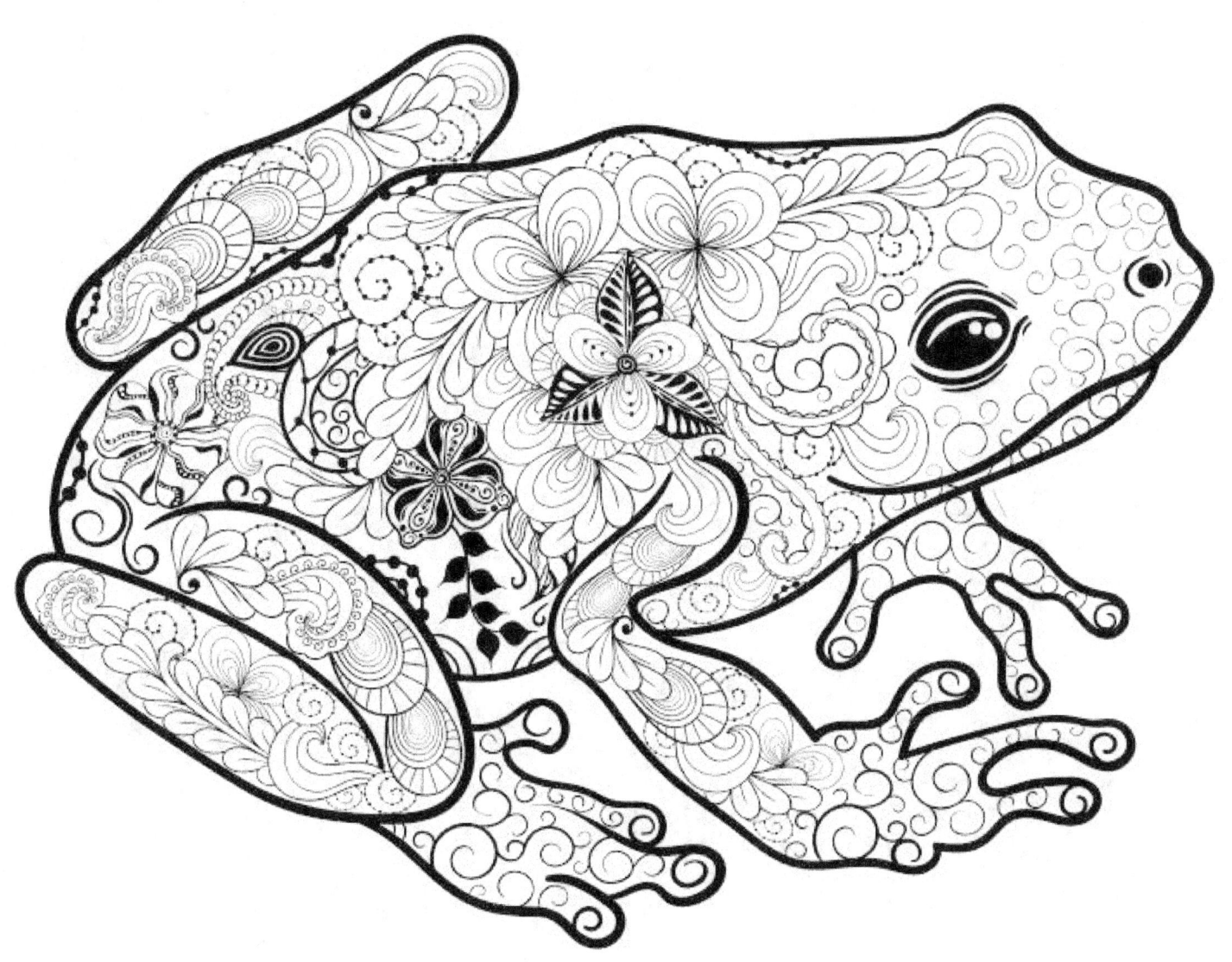

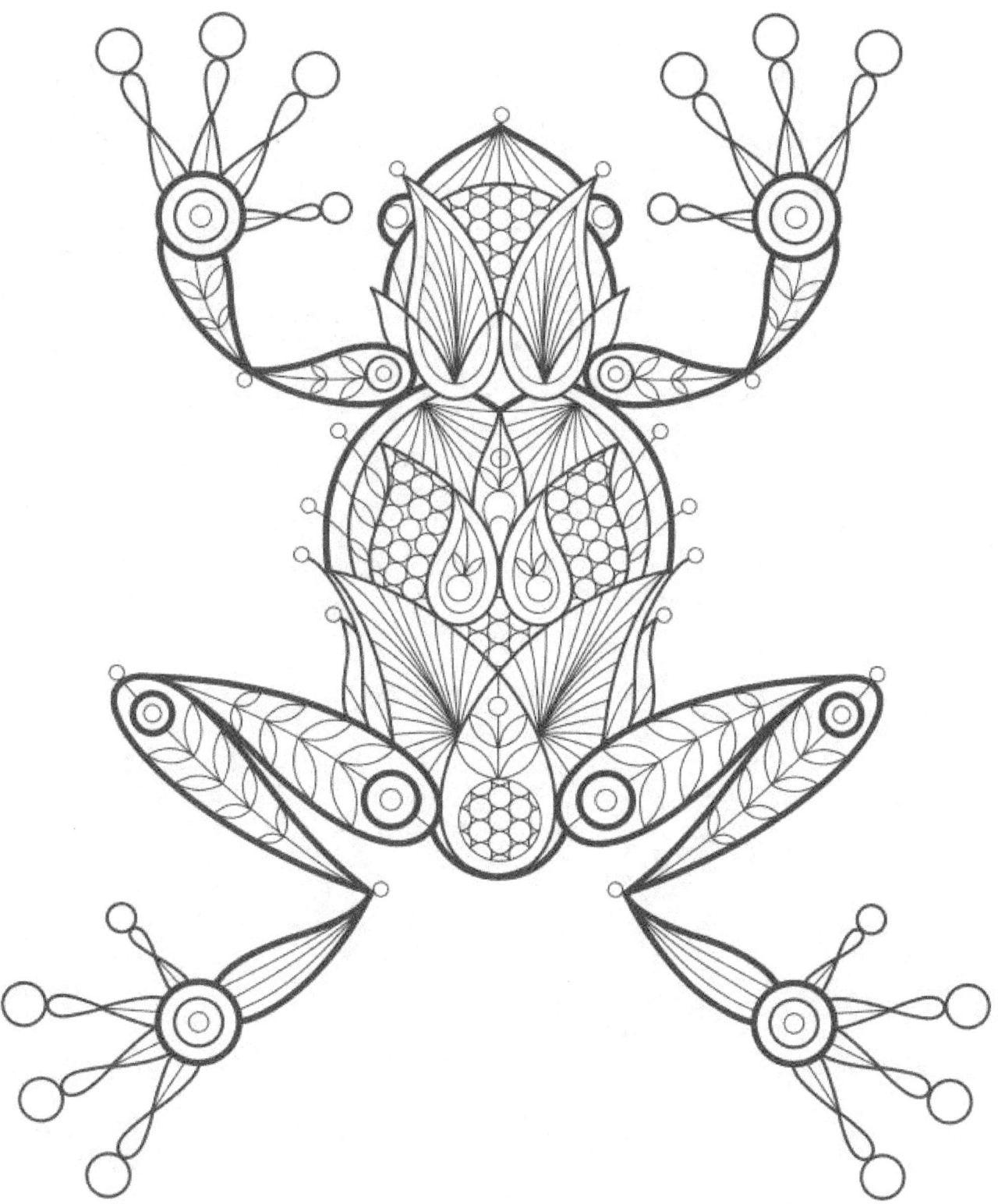

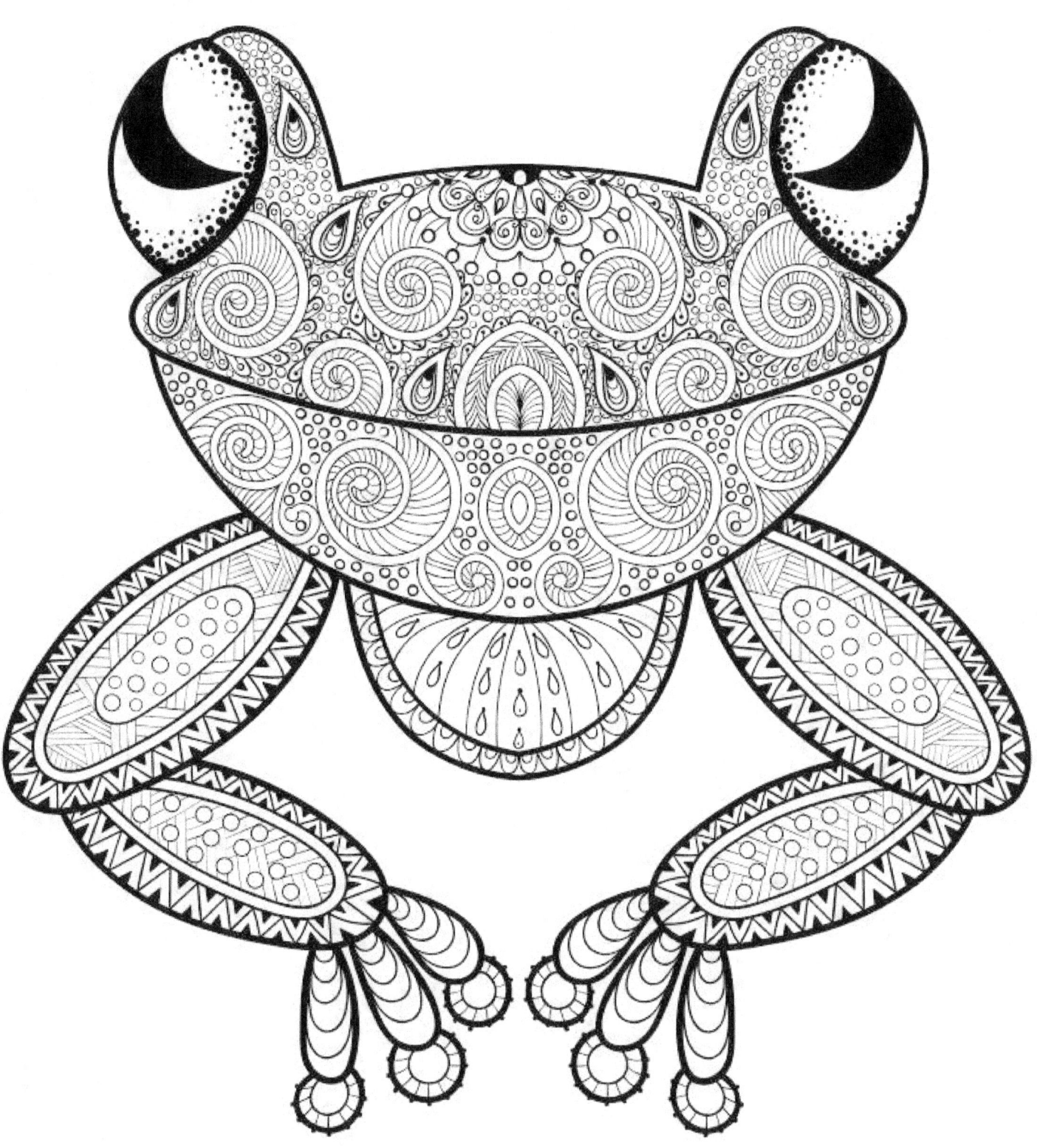

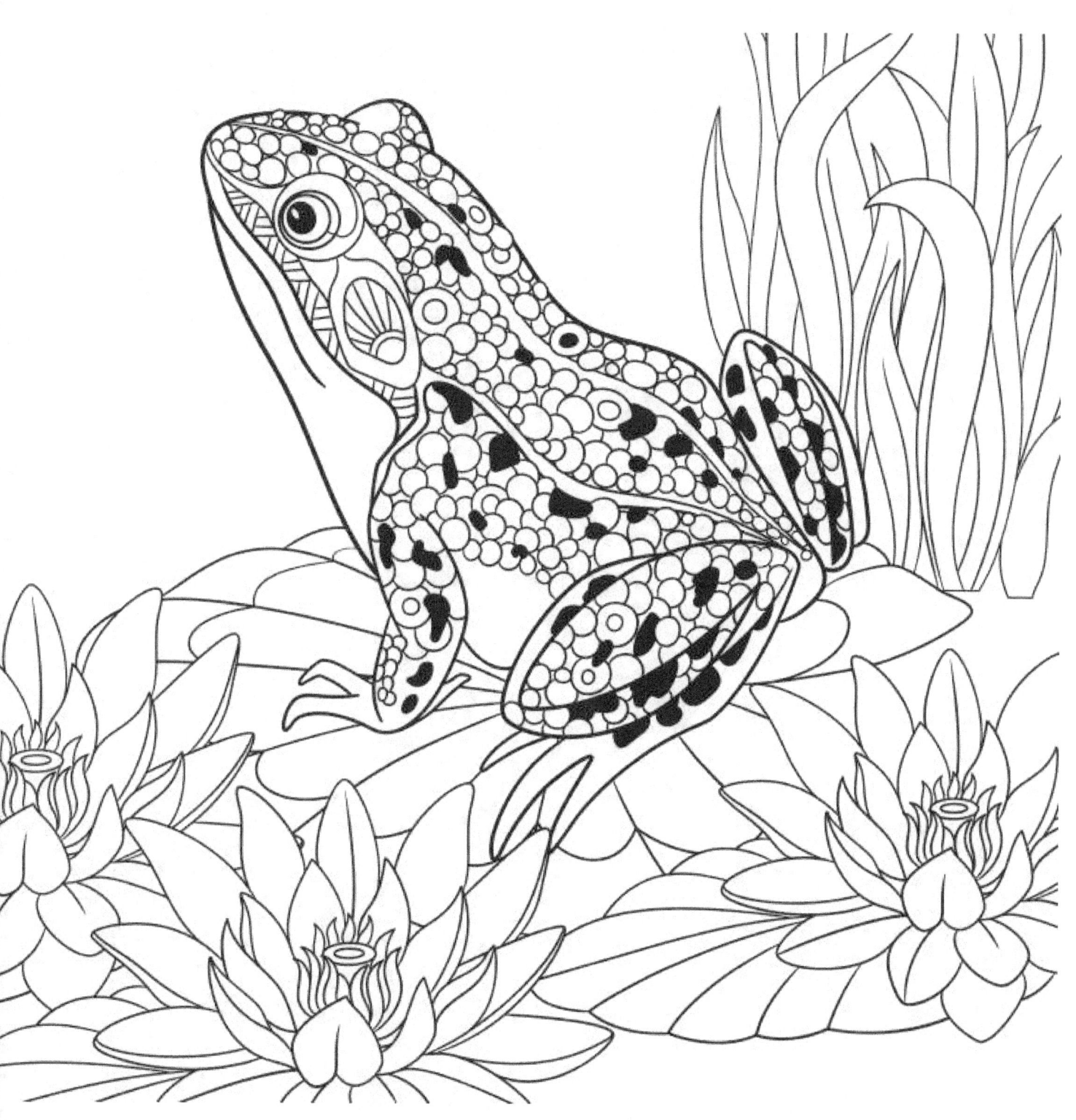

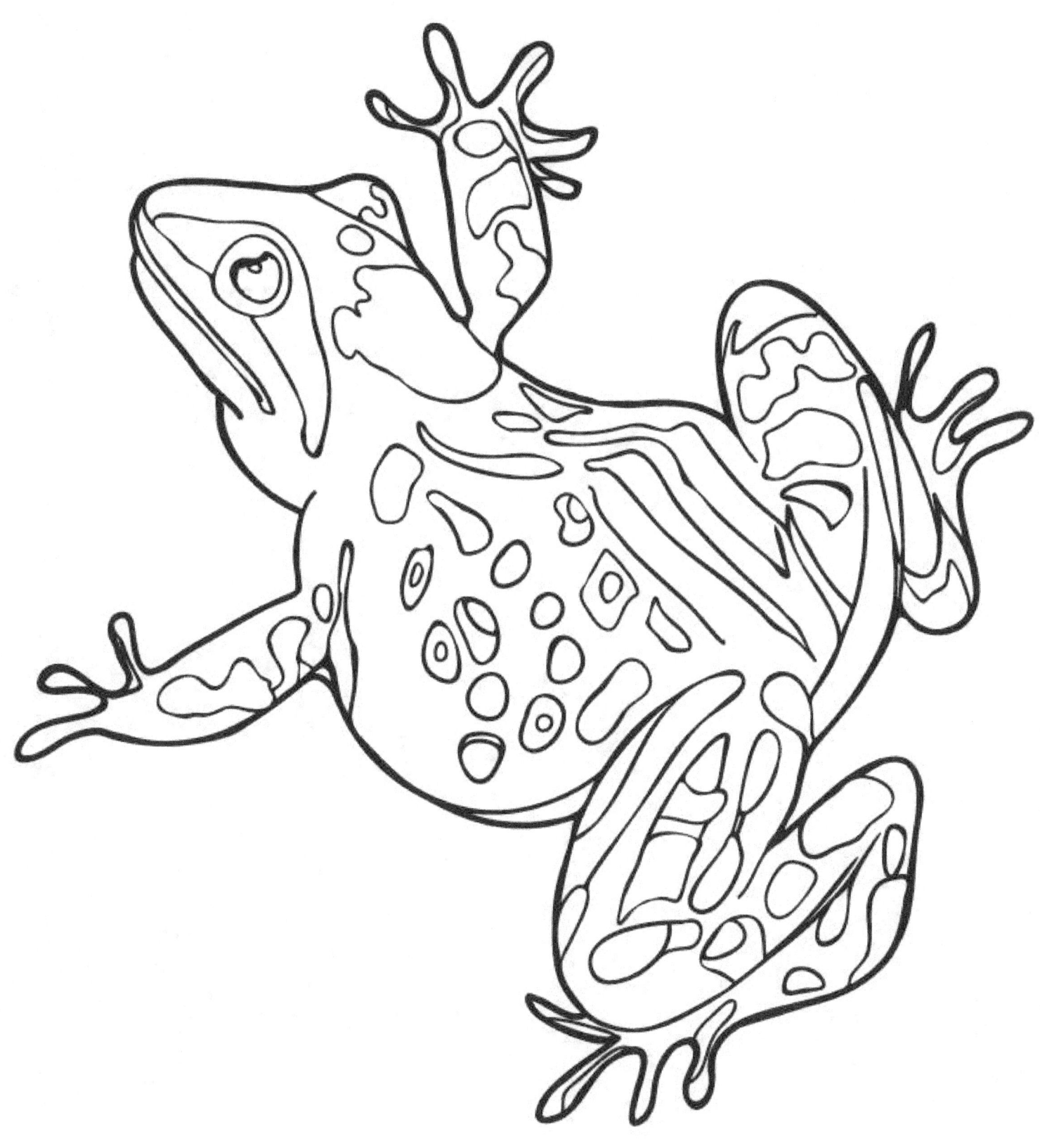

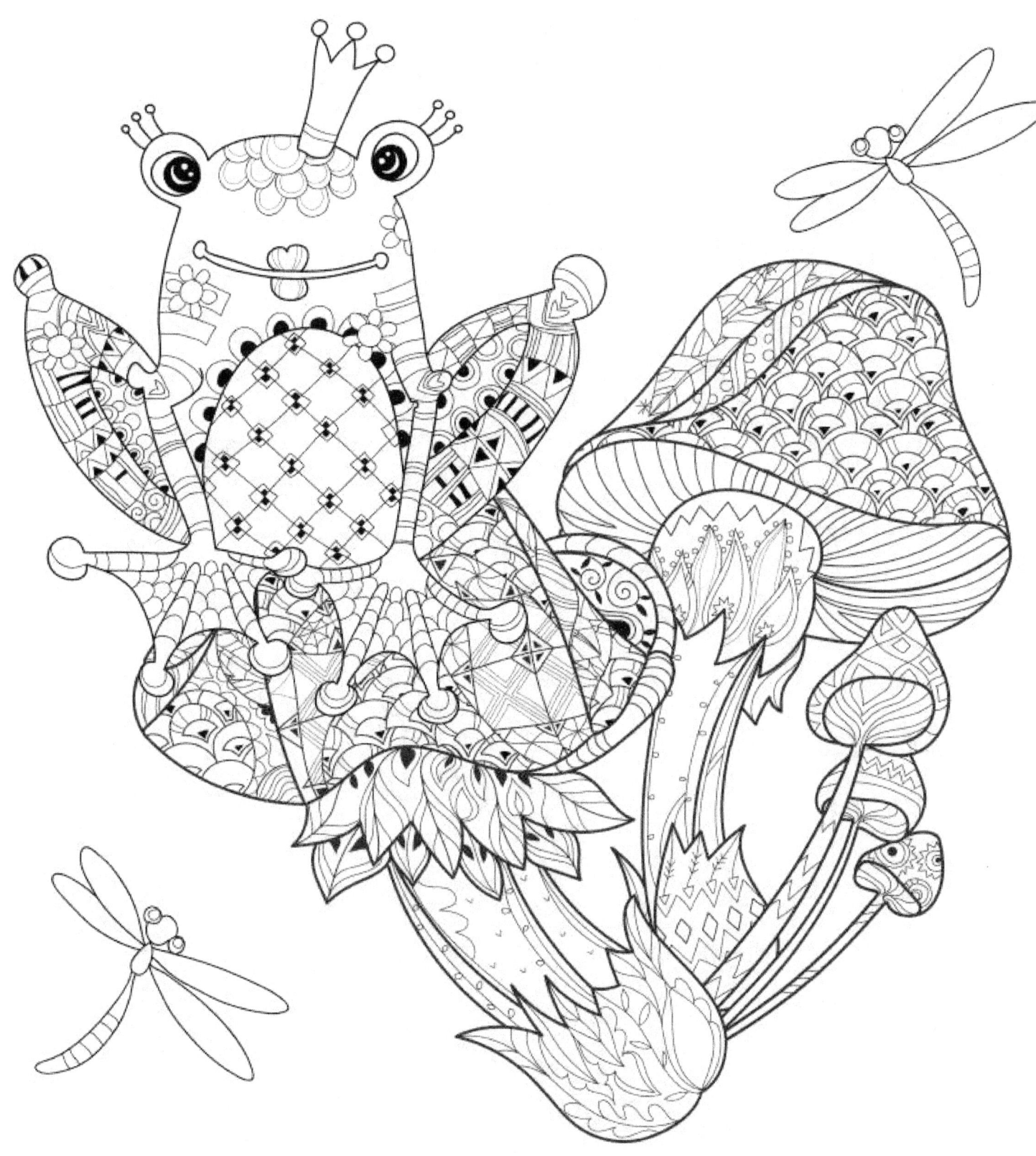

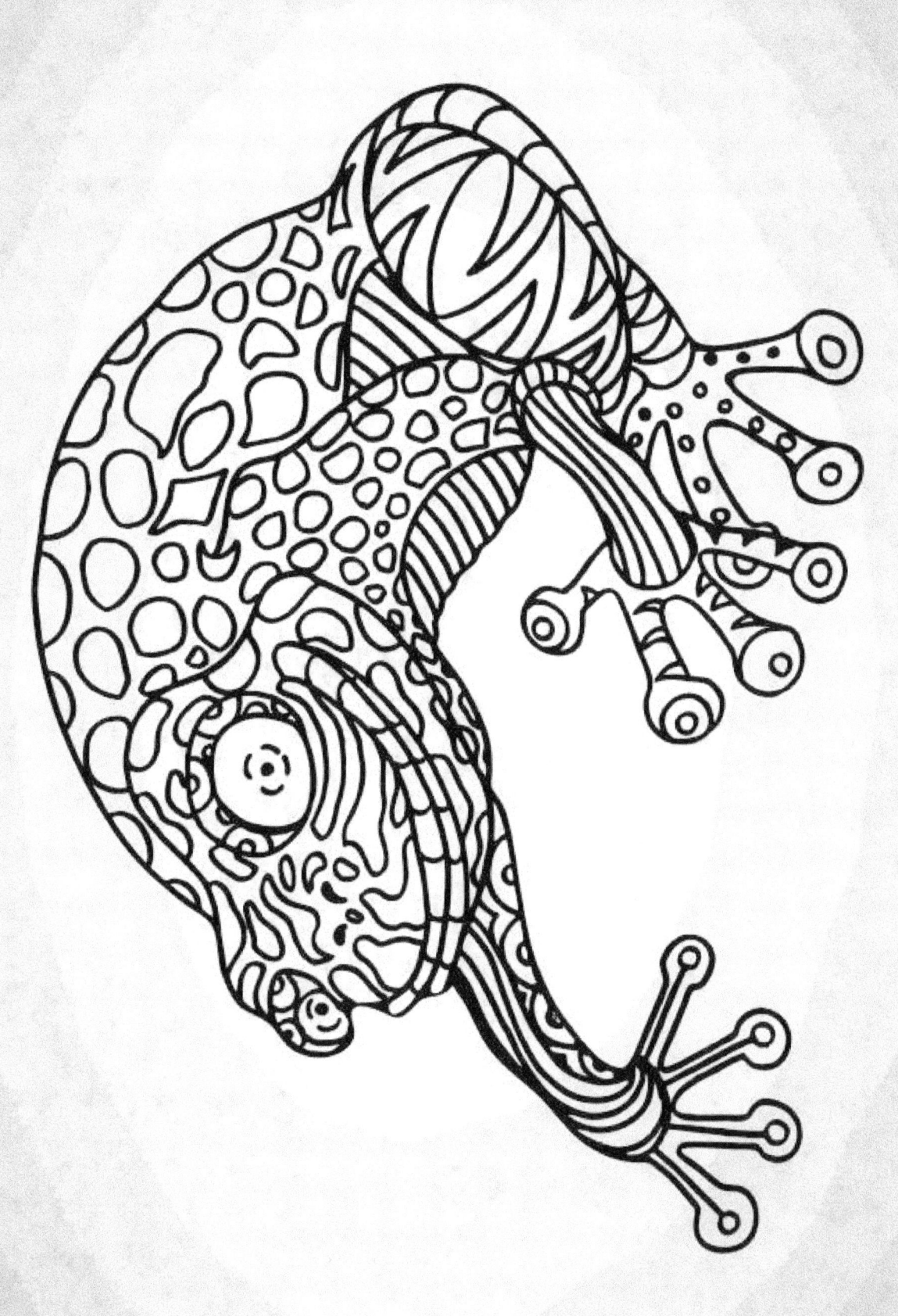

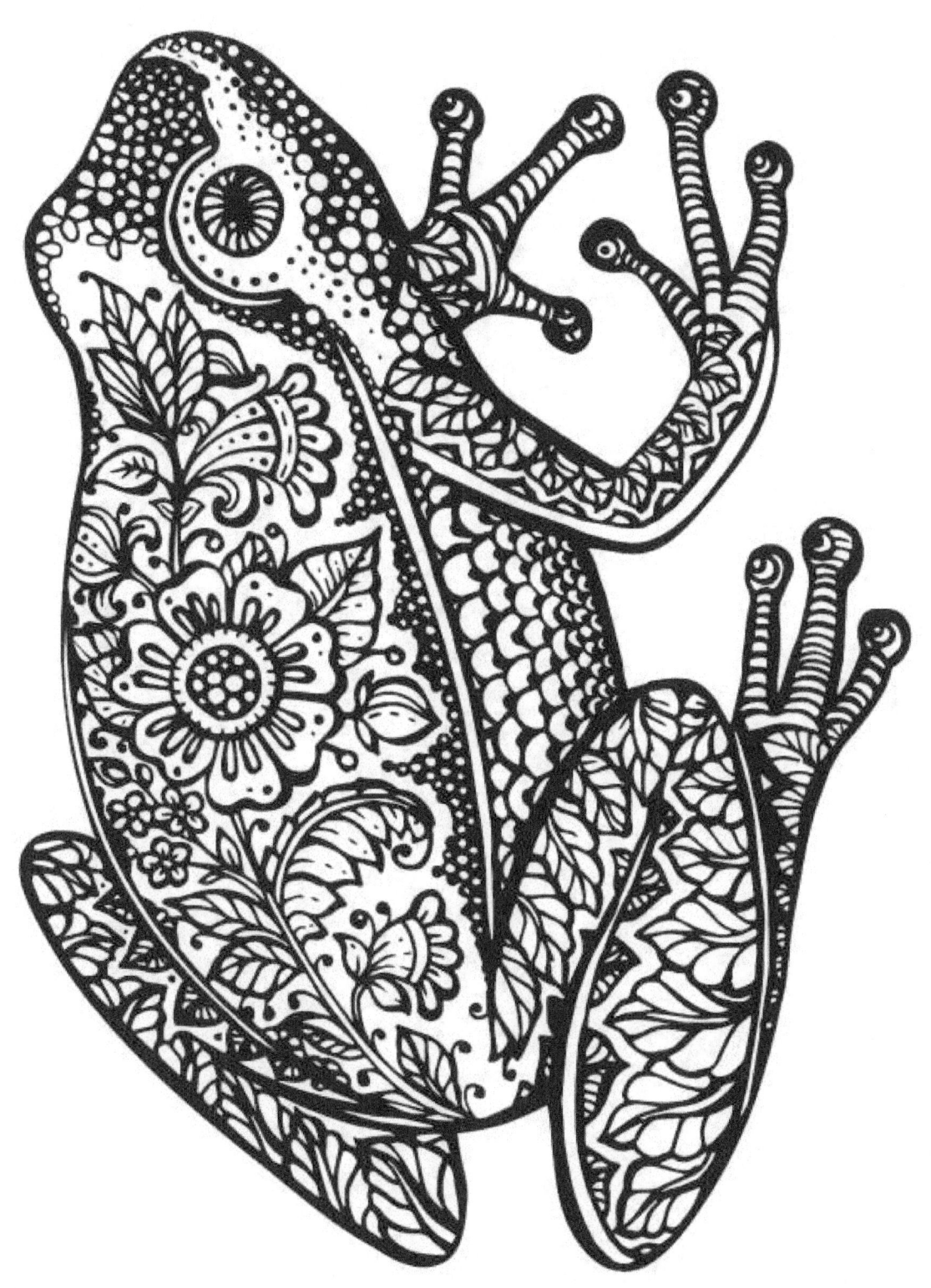

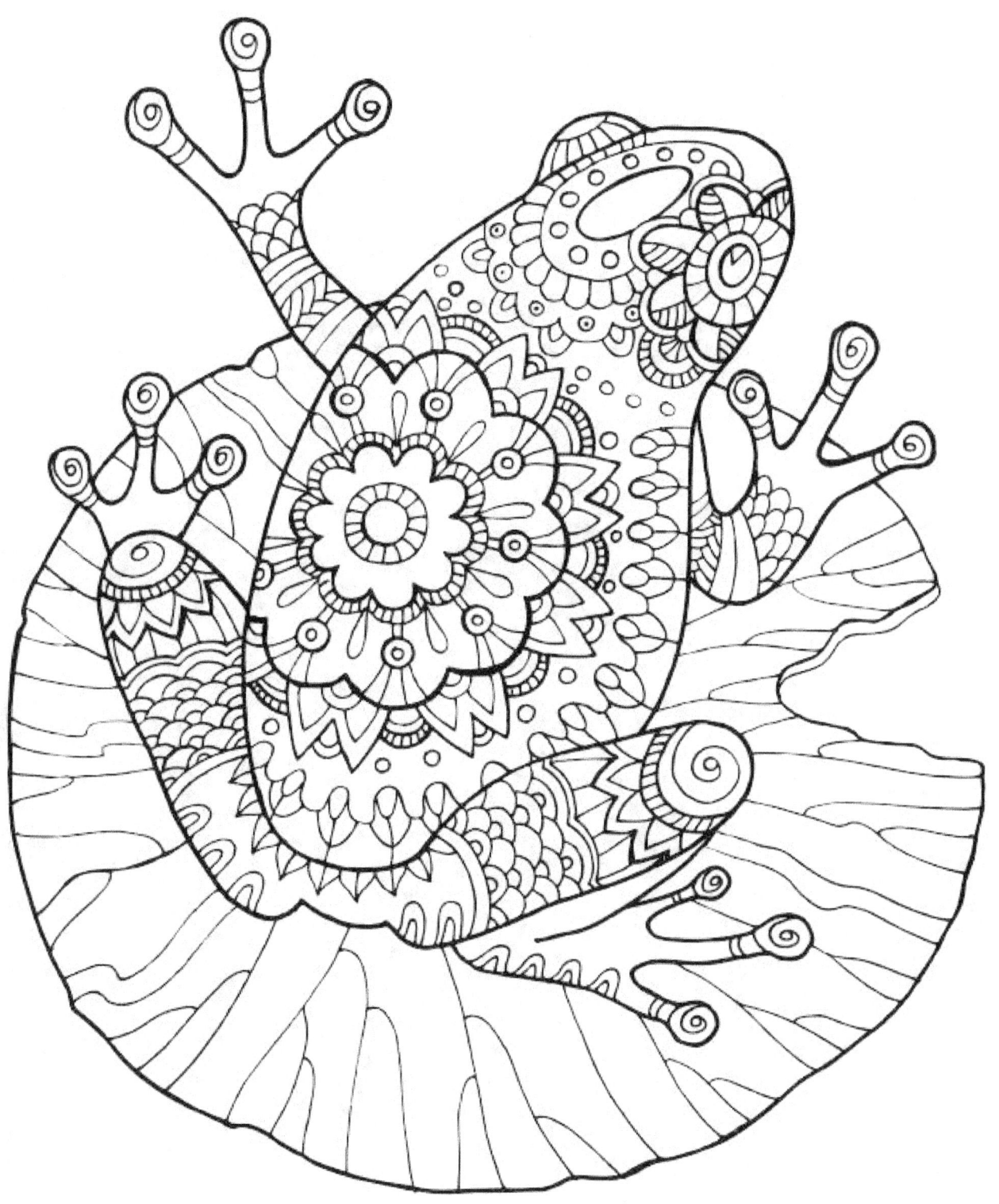

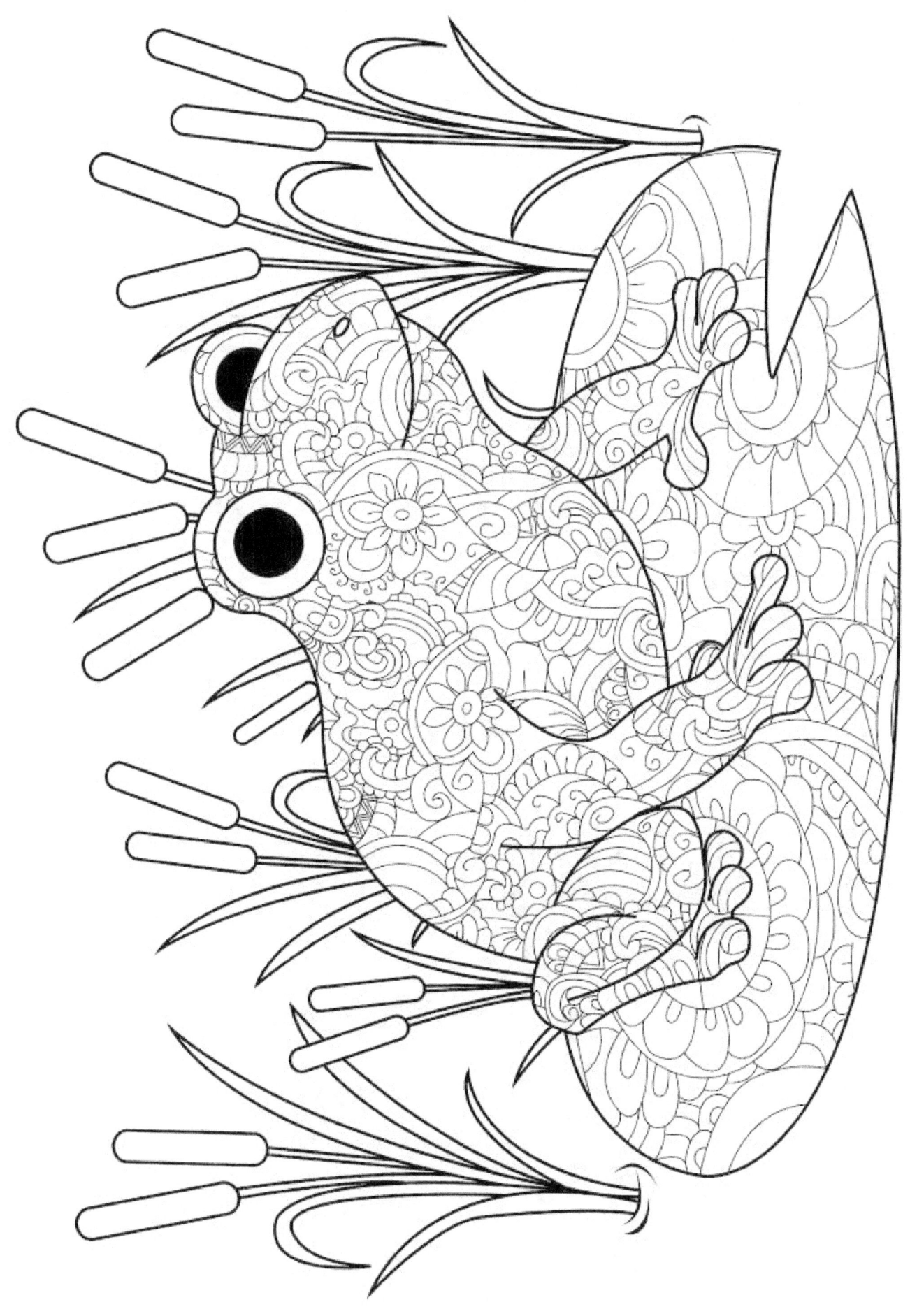

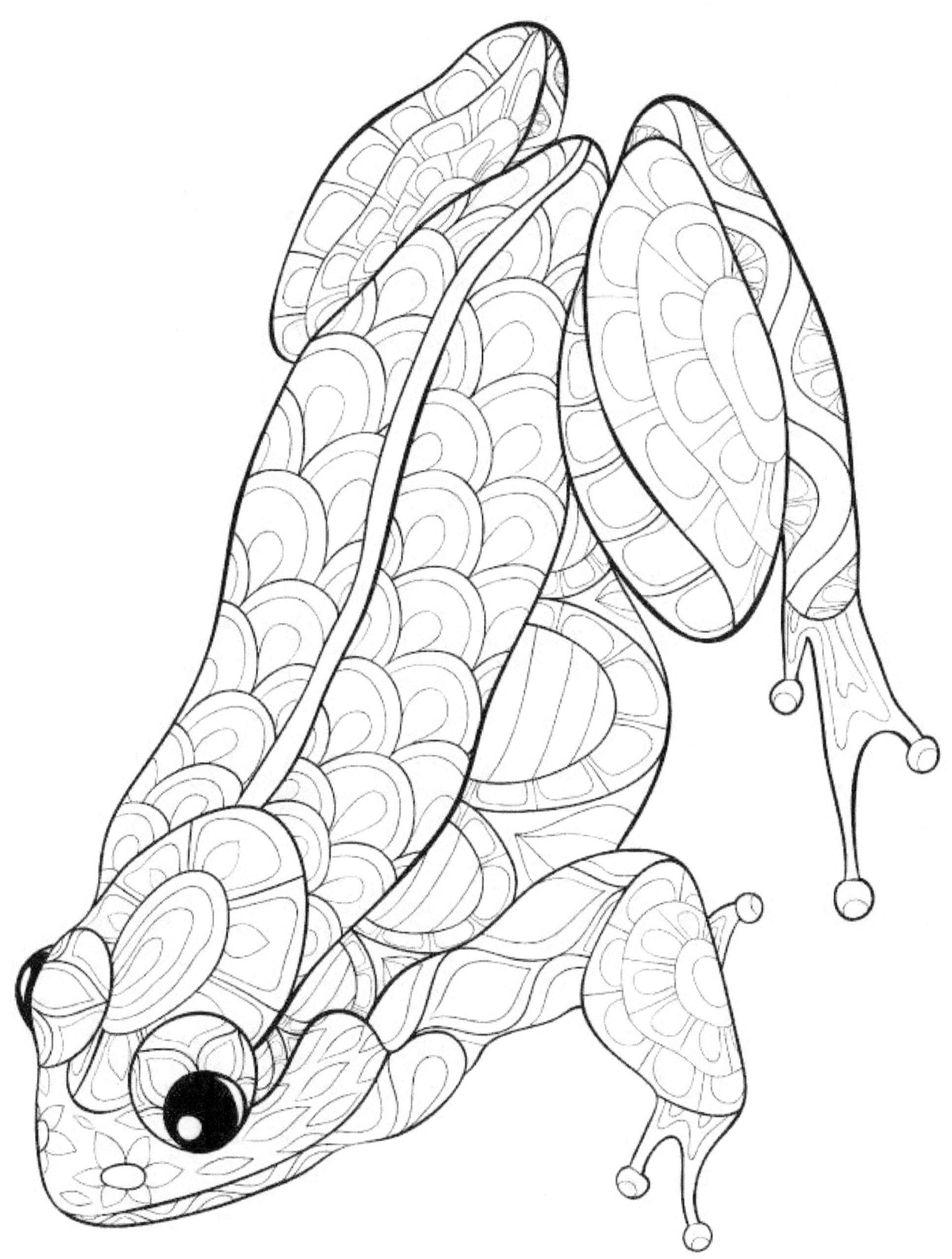

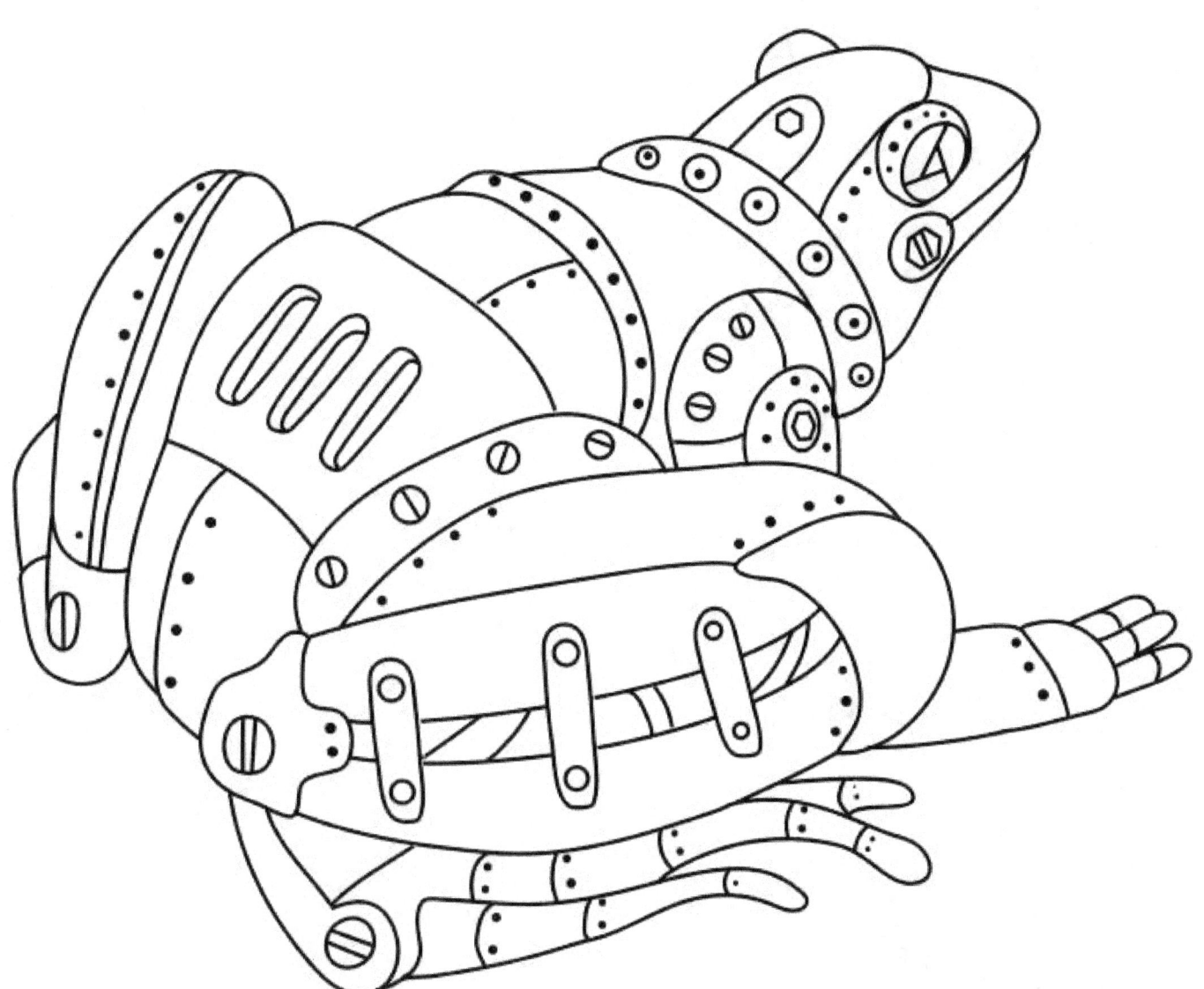

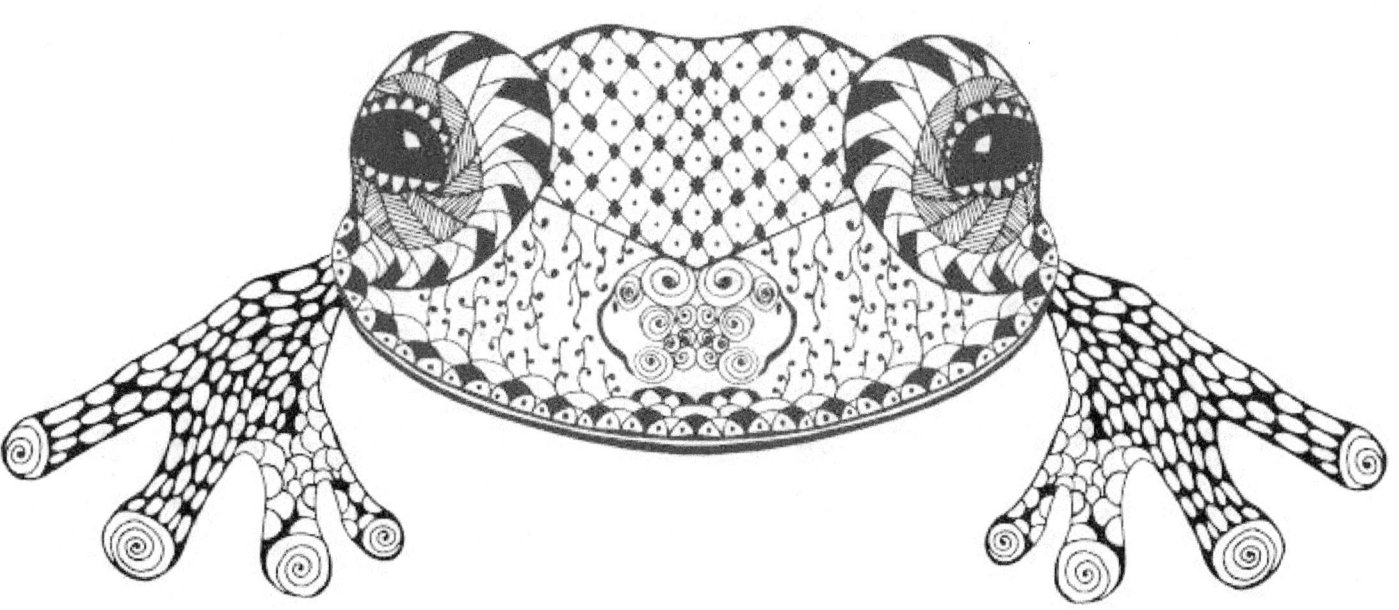

Surprise Bonus Sea Turtles Coloring Pages!

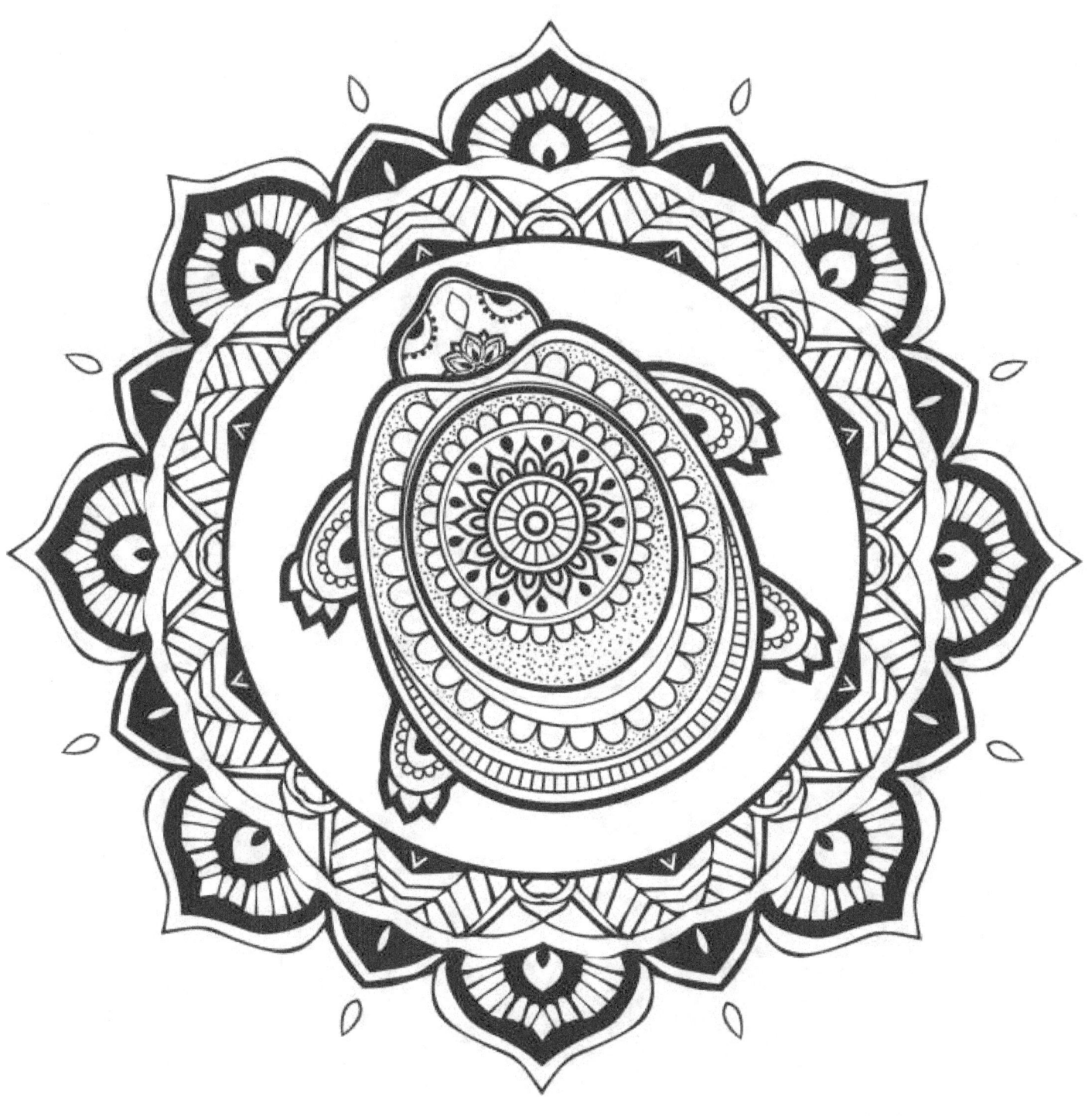

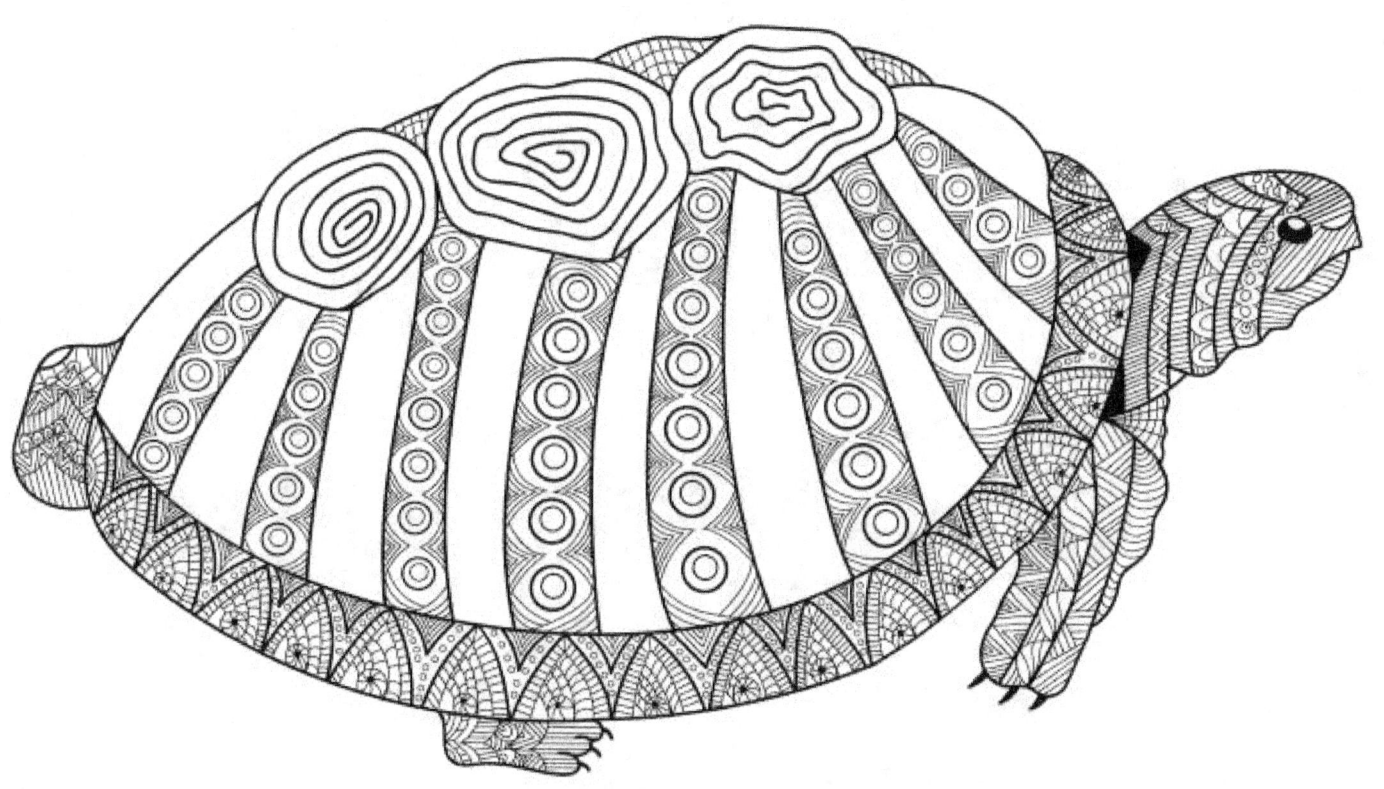

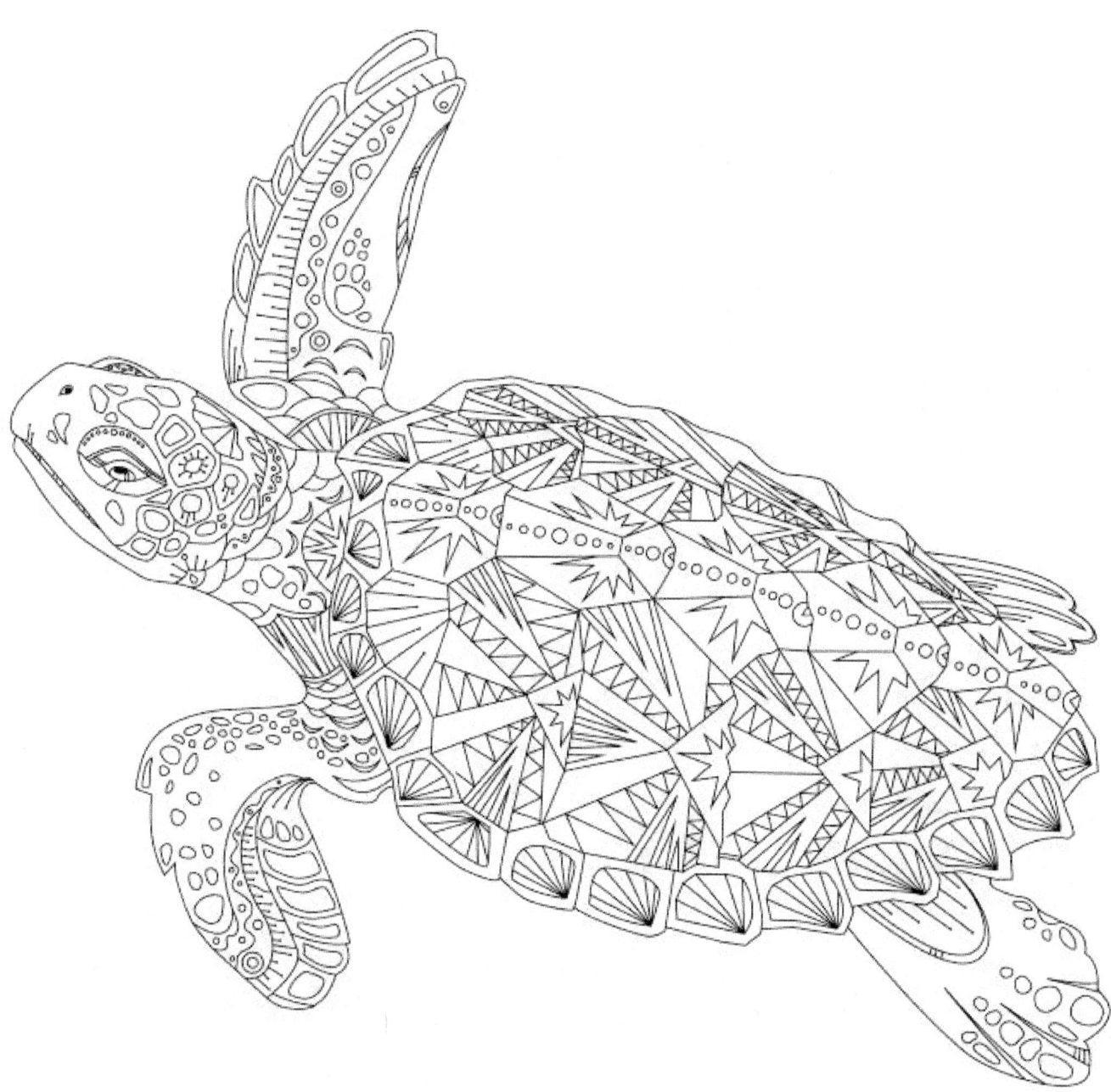

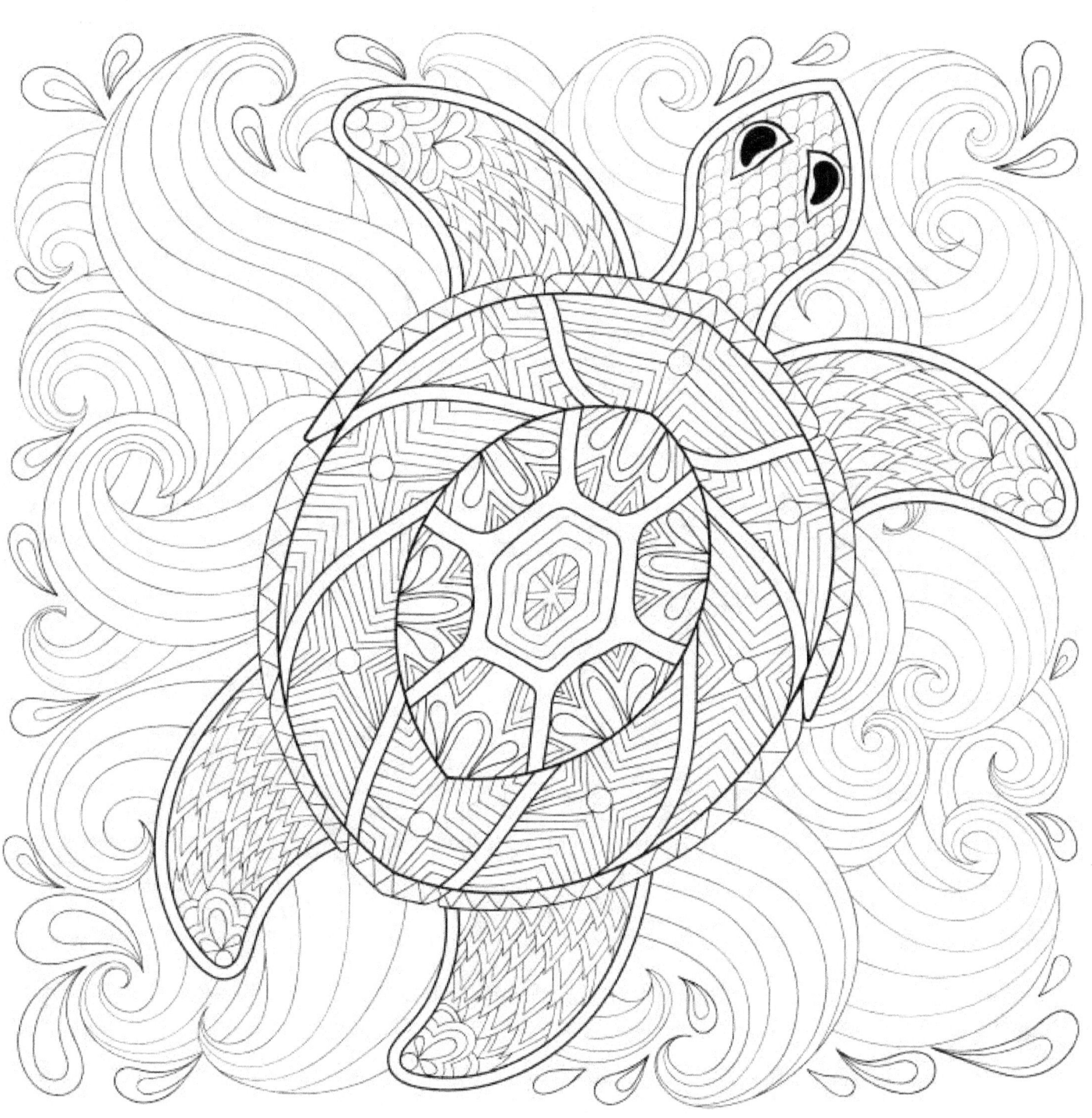

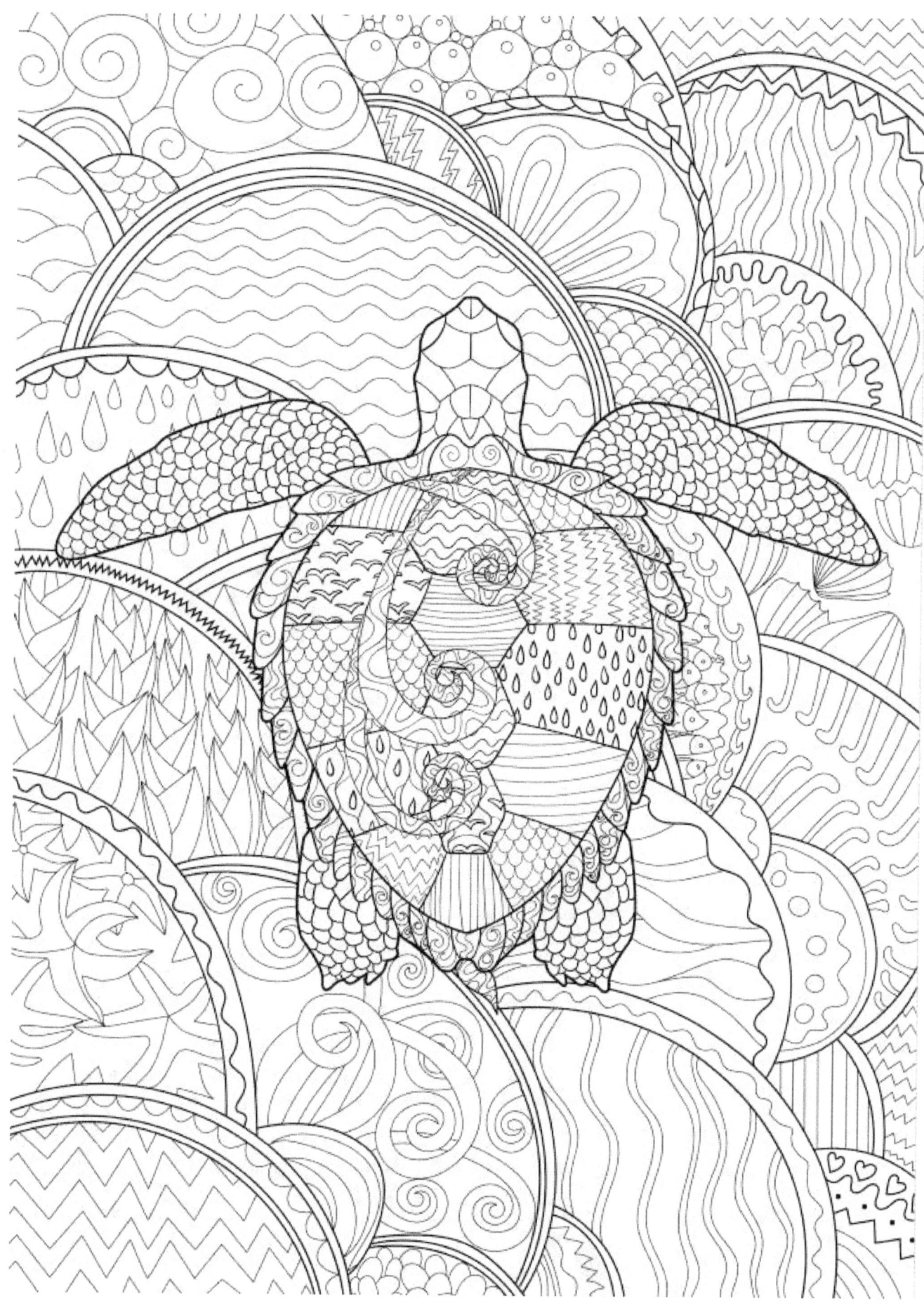

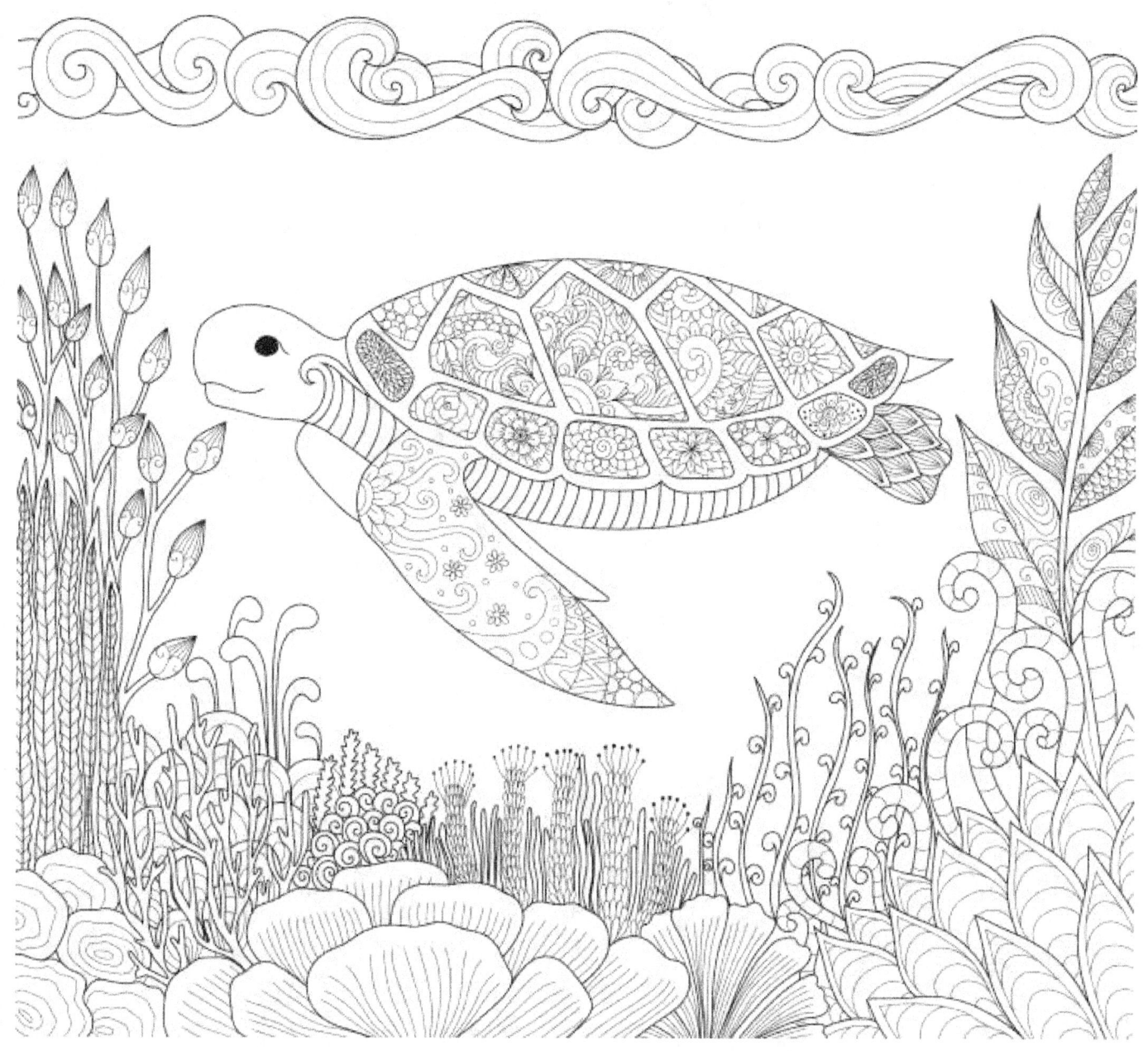

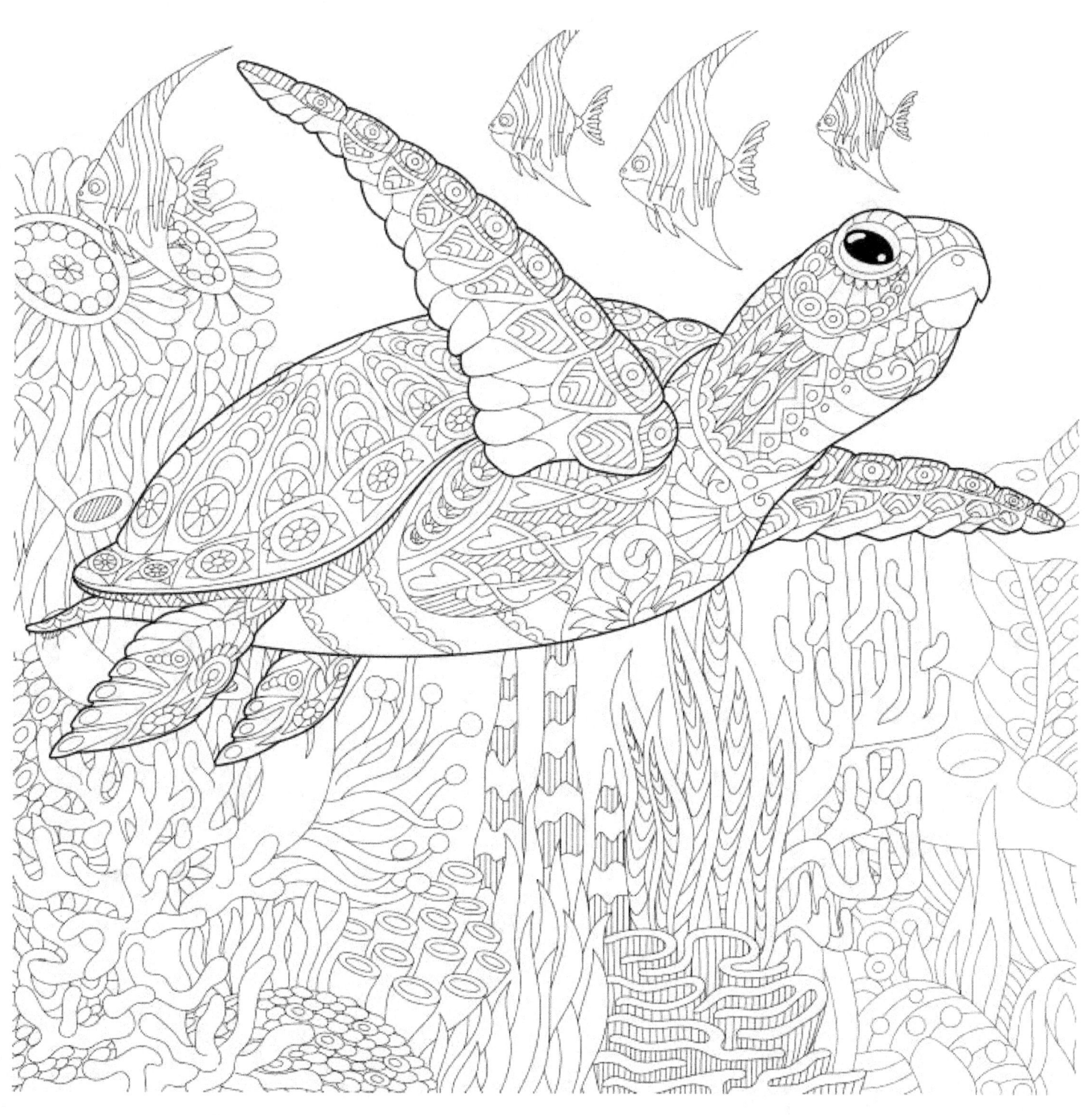

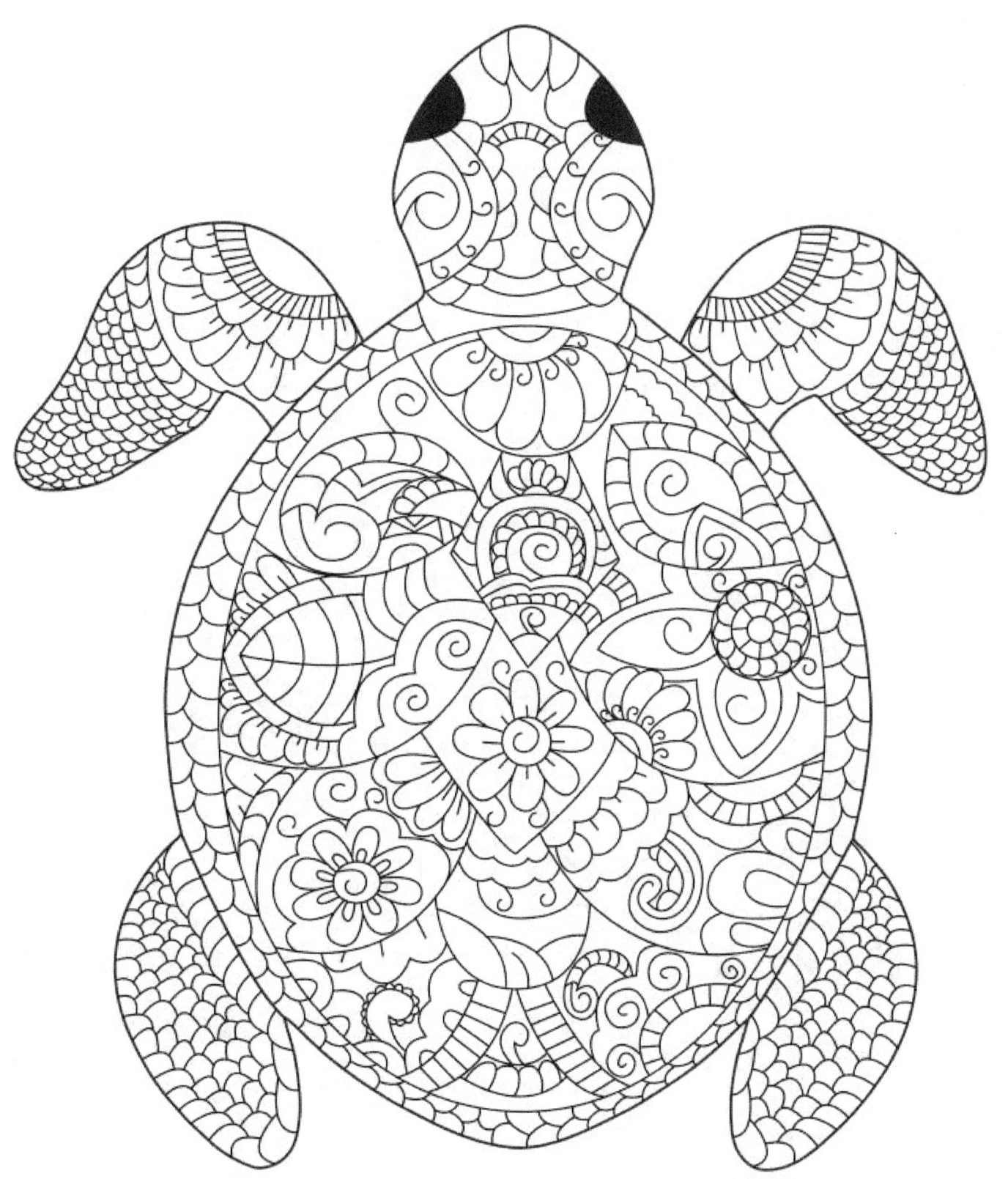

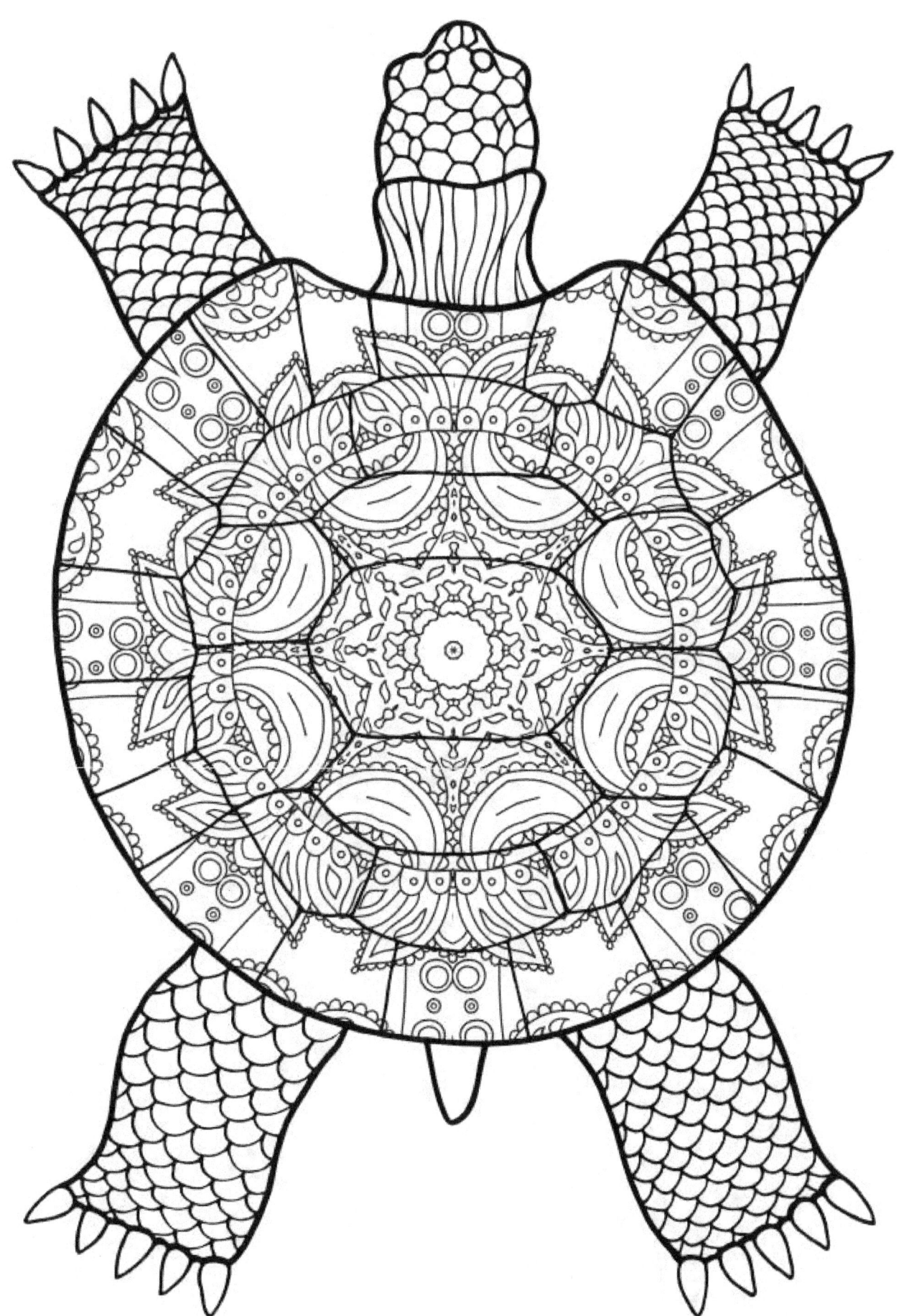